How to Start Writing
(and when to stop)

T0341660

Wisława Szymborska

How to Start Writing (and when to stop)

ADVICE FOR AUTHORS

*edited, translated, and with
an introduction by Clare Cavanagh*

A NEW DIRECTIONS BOOK

Originally published in Polish as *Poczta literacka, czyli jak zozstać (lub nie zostać) pisarzem,* ed. Teresa Walas

Published by arrangement with the Wisława Szymborska Foundation (www.szymborska.org.pl)

The Szymborska collages are from Clare Cavanagh's collection of postcards from the author and are reproduced here by permission of the Wisława Szymborska Foundation.
Excerpts from "In Praise of My Sister," "Stage Fright," and "Under One Small Star"are from *Map: Collected and Lost Poems* by Wisława Szymborksa, translated from the Polish by Stanislaw Baranczak and Clare Cavanagh. English translation copyright © 2015 by Houghton Mifflin Harcourt Publishing Company. Reprinted by permission of HarperCollins Publishers. All rights reserved.
The quotation from Rilke on p. 42 is from *Letters to a Young Poet,* translated by M. D. Herter Norton (New York: W. W. Norton & Company, 1934).

Manufactured in the United States of America
First published as New Directions Paperbook 1514 in 2021

Library of Congress Cataloging-in-Publication Data
Names: Szymborska, Wisława, author. | Cavanagh, Clare, editor, translator.
Title: How to start writing (and when to stop) : advice for writers / Wisława Szymborska ; edited, translated, and with an introduction by Clare Cavanagh.
Other titles: Poczta literacka, czyli jak zostać (lub nie zostać) pisarzem. English
Description: First edition. | New York : New Directions Publishing, 2021.
Identifiers: LCCN 2021022390 | ISBN 9780811229715 (paperback) | ISBN 9780811229722 (ebook)
Subjects: LCSH: Authorship. | Creative writing. | Feuilletons, Polish. | LCGFT: Essays.
Classification: LCC PG7178.Z9 P5813 2021 | DDC 891.8/5473—dc23
LC record available at https://lccn.loc.gov/2021022390

10 9 8 7 6 5 4 3 2 1

New Directions Books are published for James Laughlin
by New Directions Publishing Corporation
80 Eighth Avenue, New York 10011

Contents

The Use and Abuse of Poetry for Life

or, *Wisława Szymborska's do's and don't's for would-be writers*

"What would American poets and critics do without the Central Europeans and the Russians to browbeat themselves with?" Maureen McLane exclaimed in the *Chicago Tribune* some years back: "Miłosz, Wisława Szymborska, Adam Zagajewski, Zbigniew Herbert, Joseph Brodsky — here we have world-historical seriousness! Weight! Importance! Even their playfulness is weighty, metaphysical, unlike barbaric American noodlings!" For some time now, Anglo-American authors have tended to see Eastern Europe, with its twentieth-century sufferings, as a perverse promised land for modern writing, with Poland in particular serving as a kind of shorthand for "The Oppressed Country Where Poetry Still Matters." I will not attempt to speak for all the poets McLane has assembled here. Szymborska for one, though, would be shocked to find herself ranked among the metaphysically serious and universally significant world powers of modern poetry.

She celebrates the "joy of writing" in one famous lyric. She is even more persuasive on the highly underrated joy of not writing she extols in "In Praise of My Sister":

> *When my sister asks me over for lunch,*
> *I know she doesn't want to read me her poems.*
> *Her soups are delicious without ulterior motives.*
> *Her coffee doesn't spill on manuscripts.*

Szymborska is preoccupied here, as throughout her work, with the relationship between poetry and the daily life that surrounds it, feeds it, and sometimes altogether ignores it. She has nothing but sympathy for the labors of would-be writers generally: "My first poems and stories were bad too," she confesses in an interview with her friend Teresa Walas. The texts that make up her typically idiosyncratic "How to (and How Not to)" guide are culled from the advice she gave — anonymously — for many years in Literary Mailbox, a regular column in the Polish journal *Literary Life*.

She deals less gently, though, with those who scorn the sheer drudgery it takes to do anything well, be it soup-making or sonnets. "You write, 'I know my poems have many faults, but so what, I'm not going to stop and fix them,'" she chides one novice, a certain Heliodor from Przemyśl: "And why is that, oh Heliodor? Perhaps because you hold poetry so sacred? Or maybe you consider it insignificant? Both ways of treating poetry are mistaken, and what's worse, they free the novice poet from the necessity of working on his verses. It's pleasant and rewarding to tell our acquaintances that the bardic spirit seized us on Friday at 2:45 p.m. and began whispering mysterious secrets in our ear with such ardor that we scarcely had time to take them down. But at home, behind closed doors, they assiduously corrected, crossed out and revised those otherworldly utterances. Spirits are fine and dandy, but even poetry has its prosaic side." (Szymborska used the first-person plural not as the queenly prerogative of a future Nobel Laureate, but to maintain her anonymity, since Polish grammar relentlessly reveals its user's gender, and she was the only woman on *Literary Life*'s editorial staff who answered letters.)

She goes no easier on would-be novelists. "You have compiled an extensive list of writers whose talent went unrecognized by editors and publishers who later shamefacedly repented," she tells a certain Harry, from Szczecin: "We instantly caught your drift and read the enclosed feuilletons with all the humility our errors warrant. They're old hat, but that's not the point. They will certainly be included in your *Collected Works* so long as you also produce something along the lines of *David Copperfield* or *Great Expectations*."

Poor Welur from Chełm gets even shorter shrift: "'Does the enclosed prose betray talent?' It does."

Translators, for what it's worth, fare no better. "The translator must not only stay faithful to the text," she scolds H. O. from Poznań: "He or she should also reveal the poem's full beauty while retaining its form and suggesting the epoch's style and spirit. In your version, Goethe becomes a writer whose odds of achieving world glory are slim."

"True, Éluard did not know Polish" she tells Luda from Wroclaw: "But did you have to make it so obvious in your translations?"

"Poets are poetry, writers are prose," Szymborska comments in her resolutely antipoetic "Stage Fright" — or so public opinion would have it.

> Prose can hold anything including poetry,
> but in poetry there's only room for poetry —
> In keeping with the poster that announces it
> with a fin de siécle flourish of its giant P
> framed in a winged lyre's strings
> I shouldn't simply walk in, I should fly . . .

Szymborska stubbornly insists on art's "prosaic side." "Let's take the wings off and try writing on foot, shall we?" she urges the hapless Grażyna from Starachowice in one letter.

"I sigh to be a poet," exclaims Miss A. P from Białogard. "We groan to be editors," Szymborska responds, "at such moments."

She returns time and again to the mundane business of writing properly, that is to say, painstakingly and sparingly. "You need a new pen," she advises Mr. G. Kr. of Warsaw: "The one you've got keeps making mistakes. It must be foreign."

Her own favorite writing utensil, an old friend of hers once told me, was the wastepaper basket: she threw away at least ninety percent of what she wrote. My own experience bears this out. Some years back, Szymborska relayed the poems from her volume *Enough* to an international team of translators by way of her secretary, Michał Rusinek (she never mastered the Internet). We received strict instructions shortly afterward to destroy one lyric and replace it with a revised text: the final version could not coexist with what had just become the penultimate draft. I did as she asked and deleted the draft without reading it. I suspect her other translators did too. We knew the rules.

Clearly she would like more writers to follow her lead. At the very least they should equip themselves properly for the long trek ahead. "You ask in rhyme if life makes cents [*sic*]," she remarks to Pegasus from Niepolomice: "My dictionary answers in the negative."

"You treat free verse as a free-for-all," she scolds another would-be poet, Mr. K. K. from Bytom: "But poetry (whatever we may say) is, was, and will always be a game. And as every child knows, all games have rules. So why do the grown-ups forget?"

The poet's work, Szymborska remarks in her Nobel Lecture, "is hopelessly unphotogenic. Someone sits at a table or lies on a sofa while staring motionless at a wall or ceiling. Once in a while this person writes down seven lines, only to cross out one of them fifteen minutes later." But the poet's daily life is not drudgery alone. Or rather, the daily grind — the poet's or anyone's, for that matter — is anything but in the eyes and mind of an attentive writer. "Even boredom should be described with passion," she reminds Puszka from Radom: "You should start keeping a diary ... You'll soon see how many things happen even on days when nothing seems to be happening." (Her own lyric "May 16, 1973" is a case in point.)

Nonstop gloom and despair quickly wear out their welcome. "Your existential woes come a little too easily," she reprimands Bolesław L-K. of Warsaw: "'Deep thoughts,' dear Thomas says (Mann, of course, who else), 'should make us smile.' Reading your own poem 'Ocean,' we found ourselves floundering through a shallow pond. You should think of your life as a remarkable adventure that's happening to you. That is our only advice at present."

And one final remark, worth remembering perhaps when daffodils and jonquils begin to bloom once more: "We automatically disqualify all poems about spring as a matter of principle. This topic no longer exists in poetry. It continues to thrive in life of course. But that is a different matter."

"Don't bear me ill will, speech, that I borrow weighty words / then labor heavily so that they may seem light," Szymborska writes in

"Under One Small Star." She kept her own literary labors strictly off-stage. She didn't lecture on her craft. She didn't lead master classes in creative writing or devote essays to the art of verse. "I've always had the sneaking suspicion I'm not very good at it," she confesses in her — notably brief — Nobel Lecture. Not so. She was very good — but only in disguise.

Revelation through concealment shapes her own work, of course. Wit, sympathy, and others' voices combine to extraordinary effect in poem after poem: think of her Cassandra, her Byzantine mosaic, the occasional visitor from outer space. The strategic "we" she employs in *How to Start Writing (and when to stop)* does more than guide its readers through the joys — and miseries — of writing (and not writing) well. Her seriously lighthearted alter ego provides the closest look we're likely to get at the marvelous workshop in which she drafted, revised, discarded, and sometimes, mercifully, even preserved the poems that make up her small, but weighty oeuvre. "Such is life," as she warns one would-be writer: "Brief, but each detail takes time."

—CLARE CAVANAGH

How to Start Writing
(and when to stop)

To an Observer, from Krakow

You accuse us of stamping out young literary talents. "Frail seed-lings" —we read— "should be coaxed, coddled. One should not, as you do, critique their weakness, their failure as yet to yield mature fruit." We do not advocate the greenhouse cultivation of literary seedlings. Seedlings should grow in a natural environment and ac-climate to its conditions early on. Sometimes a seedling is convinced that it will be an oak while we see just an ordinary blade of grass. Even the most assiduous care will not make an oak of it. Of course our diagnoses may err at times. And so? We don't stop the seedlings from growing. We don't yank them up by the roots. They are free to mature and give proof of our error. We'll happily admit defeat. Incidentally, if you were better disposed to our column, you might notice that we are quick to praise whenever we see something worth praising. We're not to blame if this occurs infrequently. Literary tal-ent does not happen en masse.

To H. J., in Rożnica

The editors of the Mailbox receive threatening letters with some regularity. Such letters read more or less as follows: please let me know if my work is worth anything, if not, I'll pack it in, bid adieu to my dreams of greatness, descend into despair, fall prey to self-doubt, break down, take to drink, cease to believe in the meaning of my own life, etcetera. The editor does not then know how to respond. Anything he says will be taken amiss. If he says the poems or stories are bad—tragedy awaits. If he says they're good—the author fixates upon his own greatness. (This has in fact been known to happen.)

Some authors, moreover, require an immediate response, since delays may occasion dire results. (Posthaste! There's not a moment to waste.)

To Harry, from Szczecin

You have compiled an extensive list of writers whose talent went unrecognized by editors and publishers who later shamefacedly repented. We instantly caught your drift and read the enclosed feuilletons with all the humility our errors warrant. They're old hat, but that's not the point. They will certainly be included in your *Collected Works* so long as you also produce something along the lines of *David Copperfield* or *Great Expectations*.

To H. C. (or G?), from Słomniki

We request, we beg, we beseech you to pass along some legibly written manuscripts. In the meantime we keep receiving pages — worthy perhaps of dear Thomas Mann — densely covered in microscopic blots with a flourish in place of a signature. Moreover, we cannot reply in kind since the masters of the printer's craft have yet to manufacture unintelligible fonts. When that day comes, you will get our response.

To Barbara D., from Bytom

It's not just manuscripts that sometimes prove unreadable, this is true of typescripts too. You have sent what appears to be copy number ten. For mercy's sake, new eyes can't be bought even with money down.

To E. T., from Lublin

We read and read, we wade through pages black with cross-outs, and are struck by a sudden thought: why can't we be difficult for a change? Others have leeway but we don't? Why should we be dying to read something that, the evidence suggests, even the author didn't want to rewrite? Of course we have our reasons. There's always something: it's raining, Gienia is an idiot, our knee hurts, Susie has a kitty, keeping up with the Kowalskys, no one takes us to the movies, time passes, life is boring, the world will end sooner or later. Then we hunch humbly over the text once more and try to finish reading. But really there's no reason on earth to respond.

To Kryst. J., from Sędziszów

Dear Madame, we neither sell nor buy ideas. Nor do we broker such sales or purchases. Only once, from the goodness of our heart, with no ulterior motive, did we try to pitch a concept for a novel — a marketing person blows himself up. The acquaintance to whom we made this suggestion said it was over the top, nothing could come of it. We have kept our own counsel since then.

To M. Z., from Warsaw

The editor's life is full of surprises. We are expected to perform the impossible. We receive, for example, requests to provide (private) letters on what and how to write in order to be published. Others ask us to collect materials for school assignments or to write recommendations. Still others request extensive reading lists, as if writers did not require absolute independence in such matters. You have added to this litany in pleasing fashion, Mr. Z., by sending us a handful of Finnish poems (in the original) and proposing that we pick those we'd like to publish, after which you will provide us with translations. So then, the poems strike us as attractive, they are printed on quality paper, the type is crisp, the spacing and margins even, only one word crossed out in blue ink, which not only doesn't hurt the poem, it even testifies to the care with which the manuscript was prepared.

To Ata, from Kalish

These graceful little poems, replete with courtly affectations, set us to daydreaming. If we had a castle, with all its appurtenances, you would be appointed court poetess. You would mourn the distress of the rose petal on which a fly has perched unbidden, and praise the way our graceful fingers brush it from the delightful blossom. Of course, any poet who immortalized twelve uncles poisoned by cabbage stew would be flung forthwith into the dungeon for his mediocrity. The oddest thing is that the poem about the rose may be a masterpiece, while the one about the uncles comes up short . . . It's a fact, the muses are capricious and amoral. Sometimes they favor trifles. Just so long as the poet speaks in the language of his own age. Your pieces are old-fashioned in form and conceptual scope alike. This is unusual in a nineteen-year-old girl. Might you have borrowed them from your great-grandmother's album?

To Mars, from Wieliczka

Personal acquaintance with us is no one's idea of a picnic. Particularly when it comes to adepts of the pen, whom we weary with unexpected questions. For example, do they like Aristophanes, and if not, why not. Then out of the blue we inquire about some detail from Camus' *The Plague,* and a moment later we wonder out loud who wrote that comic bit about editing an agricultural gazette, who was that? Some people are troubled by such questions.

To Magro, from Krynica

Dear Sir and Madame, you ask too much of us. You both write poems and want to know which one is better. We prefer to steer clear, the more so since one sentence in your letter strikes us with terror: "Much depends on this . . ." Marital competition ends well only in comedies. Your styles, moreover, are virtually identical, hence difficult to assess. As proponents of domestic felicity, we prefer to end on this Solomonic note.

To J. Szym., from Łódź

Well, well. You carefully copied out extracts from the stories of Jan Stobierski and sent them to us with a request to print them as your debut. But this is minor compared to that titan of labor from Gdańsk who flawlessly reproduced a whole chapter of *The Magic Mountain*, changing only the characters' names by way of disguise. It came to something like thirty pages. Your paltry four pages pale by comparison. You need to get cracking. For starters we suggest *The Divine Comedy*. Not bad, and it's long.

To Wł. P., from Gdynia

We have stressed more than once how much weight we attach to these letters. A fair number of authors demand evaluation in one official-sounding sentence, clearly assuming that the texts should speak for themselves. We know nothing: not the author's age, not his education, not his profession, not his favorite books, not the standards he sets himself. In this case we don't even know if these are first efforts or if you've sent stories culled from two hundred others. To those evaluating this is no small matter. It is one thing to correct the errors of a dancer who draws literature into an intoxicating tango for the first time, and another thing entirely when the dancer in question has been treading on his partner's toes for decades. We thus request additional information.

To Il. C., from Słupsk

And now for yet another breed of letters. These too are brief and likewise contain no personal disclosures. For all this though — despite the authors' intentions — they speak volumes. We have in mind, as you must have guessed, sloppy, mistake-ridden scrawlings on worn scraps of paper. Any such letter instantly discourages further reading. It bears witness to the author's stunted aesthetic proclivities and slipshod relationship to the work. There has not been a single instance — and we've tended this Mailbox for many years — in

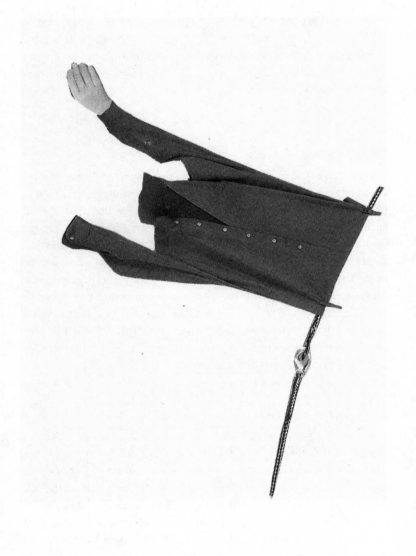

which anything worth our attention has accompanied such a letter. Not one. Each time at the end of this ill-considered calling card we feel free to stop reading.

To T. Z., from Jelenia Góra

Your letter offers still another genre that raises multiple red flags. "My letter?" you ask. "I wrote several pages! And they look just fine to me!" The letter is indeed long and carefully composed, but it says nothing. For three and a half pages its author confides that he'd been meaning to write us, that he didn't dare at first, but then decided that since he had already written it, he needed to show it to someone, and though initially he felt reluctant to send it, in the end he had to send it, since sometimes he likes what he's written, but afterwards he can't stand it, so that all he can do is to seek out an independent opinion from someone who can tell him if it was worth writing and sending or not, and so on and so forth . . . A letter of this type likewise bodes no good. We perceive instantly that the author has no sense of form, to his mind more words equal greater effect, while in point of fact he lacks both energy and imagination. In ninety-five cases out of a hundred our diagnosis proves correct; the works accompanying the letter display the same flaws. For all that we read them carefully, since that five percent still holds hope. We'll end today's survey on that note.

To Wł. T-K., from Poronin

"I apologize in advance for my orthographical errors. I was hurrying to make a clean copy . . ." This is puzzling. We'd always thought that haste adversely affects only the legibility of the handwriting. This aside, common sense advises that "horizon" may be written more speedily than "horizone," while "finish" is quicker than "finnish." In any case, what's the rush? For one thing, the world isn't due to end until mid-February. And it has yet to be confirmed that Literary

Mailbox will vanish with it. Finally, these verses thus far take the shape of scattered notes, which only the right imagination could convert into poems. We send our regards.

To O. L., from Kraków

If you lack the courage to come and talk with us about the poems you sent, why not come anyway? We welcome the timid. They generally seem to set themselves higher standards, they are more persistent and think more deeply. These qualities mean nothing in and of themselves, but in cases of innate ability they perform an invaluable service: they transform it into talent. There's no need to order a tailcoat for your visit, we are only open until noon.

To Kajka, from Radom

The editor feels acutely the hostility expressed by some past correspondents. So he takes great solace from the proposal of marriage extended in your versified letter. He sees only one obstacle, psychological, you might say. His ideal helpmate is a person who writes no poetry—even if she is glum, dim-witted, and ugly. Which is why he remains a bachelor, he's still looking.

To P. Z. D., from Chorzów

"Please give me some hope of publication, or at least provide some consolation." We must, after reading, choose the latter. So attention please, we're giving comfort. A splendid fate awaits you, the fate of a reader, and a reader of the highest caliber, that is to say, disinterested—the fate of a lover of literature, who will always be its steadiest companion, the conquest, not the conquerer. You will read it all for the pleasure of reading. Not spotting "tricks," not wondering if this or that passage might be better written, or just as well, but differently. No envy, no dejection, no attacks of spleen, none of the sensations accompanying the reader who also writes. For you

Dante will always be Dante, whether or not he had aunts in the publishing business. You will not be tortured at night by the question of why X., who writes free verse, gets published, while you, who rhyme relentlessly while counting syllables on both hands, don't even merit rejections. The editor's facial expressions will mean less than nothing to you, while the wincing at various stages will signify, if not nothing, then at least not much. And there is also this not inconsiderable benefit: people speak of incompetent writers, but never of incompetent readers. There are of course hordes of failed readers—needless to say, we do not include you among them—but somehow they get away with it, whereas anyone who writes without success will instantly be deluged in winks and sighs. Not even girlfriends are to be relied upon in such cases. So how do you feel now? Like a king? We should hope so.

To Marlon, from Bochnia

Not everyone who can draw a sitting cat, a little house with smoke coming from the chimney, or a face consisting of a circle, two lines and two dots is destined to become a great painter. For the moment, dear Marlon, your poems are on the level of such sketches. Keep writing, think about poetry, read poetry, but also consider acquiring practical know-how independent of the muses' patronage. They are hysterical, and hysterics are notoriously unreliable.

To H. W., from Warsaw

Knock writing out of his head? Don't even think about it. In the first place, the situation will take care of itself in a couple of years. Secondly, the boy enjoys poetry so much that he rejects other forms of amusement out of hand. That said, we do not advise steering him toward more suitable reading. Suggestions would make sense only if the young man displayed no humanistic proclivities and planned on becoming a technical nitwit. This does not appear to be the case. Let him select his own reading (he's doing this anyway), he's learning to choose, and if he picks a book beyond his years, don't worry, just secretly read the book yourself so as to be prepared for future conversations. Not talking about books is not an option.

To Z. Z., from Łódź

You took our response as a personal affront. You shouldn't have. Really. In stating that you lack imagination, so crucial to poetry, we cast no aspersions upon your merits of character and heart, your fitness for your chosen trade, your intellectual horizons, your manners, your manhood—in short, at no point do we overstep our limited editorial privileges. The romantic notion that writing poetry yields the greatest honor and glory may persist, but in truth the greatest honor and glory lies in doing whatever you're best equipped to do beautifully. With best wishes.

To Nowogard

A literature major prepares you chiefly for a teaching career, it will not show you how to write good poems. No course, however scrupulously attended, creates talent. At best it fosters a talent that already exists. You have written a charming little poem, which comes easily to someone just discovering first love. All lovers manifest one fleeting talent or another. Alas, though, such talents rarely withstand the test of the heart's discontinued affections. So Eva, have you considered chemistry?

To W-icz, from Lublin

Sometimes fate allots just enough literary talent to permit the writing of fine letters. In reality, though, no one writes letters these days, we phone our friends, and even friendly conversation no longer includes the art of exchanging views. As a result, this small, but worthy talent can't find the appropriate outlet. The one it finds is false: it hammers away at poetry and prose in the mistaken belief that what may interest a friend or relation will likewise engage a mass reader-ship. Our advice is old-fashioned: find a sympathetic correspondent with whom you may discuss larger topics. Who knows, perhaps the custom of composing lengthy letters may come back. You will then be avant la lettre.

To B. K., from Goleniów

"In heaven's midst the Milky Way, / Across celestial paths it lays / Sprawling like a lacy shawl . . ." — We find it hard to believe that you are already eighteen, we'd have guessed more like twelve, since you still don't seem to have opened even the humblest handbook on the stars. We suspect that just one such book would make this poem seem childish, and the shawl to which you compare the Milky Way would look like a scarf draped carelessly across your great-grand-mother's armoire. If you are in fact eighteen, then the writing of verse might best be left to others. Don't envy them, though, they've got a tough row to hoe.

To M. D.

You have doubtless taken the opportunity to recite these charm-ing rhymes at some local ceremony, after the official program of course, the great speeches and Chopin's polonaise as played by a chubby-cheeked child in pink hairbows. The audience settles in its seats and wonders what's next, maybe time to head for the buffet? Then suddenly these poems about our town. The author mentions everyone by name, so obligingly, so politely. Outbursts of laugh-ter and applause. The ill-fated moment comes later. Someone tells the author: "You should publish them, it's a shame to waste them." Alas, this advice is not sound. The laurels were not in vain, they delighted all concerned. Only now are they wasted, in the editors' office, where they are weighed on literary scales. These will say they are not poetry, and give the author great pain. Which could have been avoided.

To W. K., from Lublin

Your observations thus far are purely private in nature—they concern people and places sketched in such a hazy, disjointed way that they fail to draw the reader's attention. Incidentally, we don't understand why you speak of your mania for writing as if it were some shameful disease of which you must be cured posthaste. There is nothing remotely abnormal in wanting to jot down your thoughts and experiences. On the contrary—this reveals personal literary culture. Which is obligatory not only for authors, but for educated people generally. When we read published versions of memoirs and letters, we marvel at the literary form these self-disclosures take—composed as they so often are by individuals who not only were not writers, but had no intention of becoming writers . . . These days, though, no sooner does someone jot down a few words than he or she begins to weigh their value, is obsessed by thoughts of publication, wonders if the time has been well spent . . . It's a shame that every more or less gracefully formulated sentence must pay off instantly. What if the payoff comes only ten or twenty years later? And what if this well-wrought phrase never reaps dividends in any public sense, but supports the writer in dark hours and enriches his life? Does that count for nothing?

To Halina W., from Białystok

We'll begin with something shocking: you are too artless and pure to write well. Various demons inhabit the abysses of a gifted writer. They may (or should) doze before and after writing, but they stir up all kinds of trouble in the interim. Without their assistance the writer couldn't penetrate the dense emotional thickets of his many characters. Nothing human is alien to him—and it's not just well-behaved saints' lives that hide beneath this adage. Faithfully yours.

To H. C., from Kraków

Lack of literary talent is no disgrace. Many wise, noble, enlightened souls, immensely gifted in other fields, have likewise suffered. In saying that the text is second-rate, we intend no offense, we have no wish to strip the meaning from your existence. It must be admitted, though, that we do not always express our opinions with Chinese politeness. Oh, the Chinese, they really knew—at least before the Cultural Revolution—how to let less fortunate poets down. The answer would run something like this: "The honored gentleman's poems surpass everything hitherto written and everything to be written hereafter. Were they to appear in print, all literature would pale in their dazzling light, and other practitioners of the art would painfully recognize their own insignificance . . ."

To J. W., from Warsaw

We worry when a novice author, having placed his first poem in some journal, abandons his studies to live solely by and for poetry. As a rule, the outcome is as follows: a year of college is lost for good, while subsequent poems spend months in editors' offices, waiting—at best—for a chance to appear in the columns of some periodical or other. We offer fatherly advice: be prudent, especially since your poems thus far are merely correct, and the poets' road to hell is, as we know, littered with such compositions. What are you giving up anyway, medicine? Friedrich Schiller's profession?

To a Seeker, from Kudowa

No, we don't have any guides for writing novels. We hear such things appear in the United States, but we make bold to question their worth for one simple reason: wouldn't any author who possessed a fail-proof recipe for literary success rather profit from it himself than write guidebooks for a living? Right? Right.

To Waldemar, from Kraków

Of course you can suddenly start writing after forty. That's not even particularly late, given that other laws govern such mature beginnings. A youthful debut succeeds by way of imaginative freshness and a still unfettered worldview. Impressions, not reflections, dominate; spontaneous observations take the place of insights drawn from a hard-won understanding of the world. From a late debut, on the other hand, we expect additional virtues: a fair share of human experience and—in cases not involving fact-based memoirs—a consciously shaped literary taste. In a word, a forty-year-old shouldn't write as if he or she were seventeen, since then neither time nor mental gifts will take up the slack.

To U. T., from Kraków

A young musician attends the conservatory, a young artist studies at the academy, but the young writer has nowhere to go. You view this as an injustice. Not so. Schools for musicians and painters provide first and foremost technical knowledge you'd be hard-pressed to acquire on your own in relatively short order. What is the writer to learn at his institute? Any ordinary school is all it takes to push a pen across the page. Literature holds no technical secrets, or at least secrets that can't be plumbed by a gifted amateur (since no diploma will help the talentless). It's the least professional of all artistic callings. You may take up writing at twenty or seventy. You may be a professor or an autodidact. You may skip your high school diploma (like Thomas Mann) or receive honorary doctorates at multiple universities (again like Mann). The road to Parnassus is open to all. In principle at least, since genes have the final say.

To Eug. Ł., from Inowrocław

The same old complaint about "youth." This time we're supposed to forgive the author since he still hasn't been anywhere, experienced anything worth mentioning, or read everything that he should. Such confessions betray the belief (adolescent, hence a bit simplistic) that external circumstances alone make the writer. That his creative quality derives from the quantity of his life adventures. In fact, the writer develops internally, within his own heart and mind: through an innate (we repeat, innate) propensity for thought, acute sensitivity to minor matters, astonishment at what others see as ordinary. Trips abroad? We sincerely hope you'll take them, they sometimes come in handy. But before you head off to Capri, we suggest a trip to Lesser Wólka. If you come back with nothing to write about, then no azure grottoes will save you.

To Tede., from Chełm, Lublin Province

Of course, real talent requires tips and pointers, especially to start. But these lessons should come easily, almost incidentally. A genuine sense for what's better or worse aesthetically, what's more or less important, what works, or doesn't, and why: it is not simply a matter of wide reading and familiarity with various -isms. It is above all instinct. We take the liberty of saying this after long years of observation. A few comments on a flawed metaphor may keep one novice poet from making the same mistake twice. A whole day's conversation won't help another. That same instinct will draw the beginner to those who know more than he does, who surpass him in experience, sensitivity and culture. Such people may be found wherever you look for them. We are not asking you to drop your current friends, we simply doubt that they suffice. From your letter we gather that your heart may be taken, but that your head is still up for grabs.

To W. J., from Kraków

If you are eighteen, please pass on your next efforts in a year's time. If you're twenty-five, please send posthaste any stories you've kept hidden in your desk drawer. If you've already reached thirty—we wish you enjoyment in the bosom of your friends.

To Z. H., from Szczecin

You like the idea of the "little man." All the characters in the stories you've sent are the same: colorless, drab, blurry. This worries us, since literature holds no place for such heroes. People all look the same only from a distance, while a writer must observe up close. "Must"—but that's not the right word, no one's going to arrest him, it's simply a matter of writerly instinct. We can't really sympathize with Manuel as he wanders from table to table muttering "life is meaningless," since we have no clue as to what drove him to this categorical conclusion. Did his girl drop him for no reason? But she had her reasons, she did: he's a snore.

To Ula, from Sopot

A definition of poetry in one sentence—please. We know at least five hundred from various sources, none of which strike us as both all-embracing and pleasingly precise. Each expresses the taste of its own age. Our native scepticism saves us from attempting new definitions. But Carl Sandburg's lovely aphorism comes to mind: "Poetry is a diary kept by a sea creature who lives on land and wishes he could fly." Will that do for now?

To Ir. Przyb., from Gdańsk

Please stop trying to be poetic at any price, the poetical is dull since it's always secondhand. Poetry, like all literature for that matter, derives its vital energies from the world we live in, from events experienced, trials endured, ideas conceived. The world must always be described anew, since it is never what it used to be, if only because we ourselves are new to it. Swinburne could have written your poem "Wuthering Wind." But you're only twenty-four and thirty million compatriots wait with bated breath to hear what you've got to say.

To Pal-Zet, from Skarżysko-Kam.

After reading the enclosed verses we conclude that you don't sense the fundamental difference between poetry and prose. The poem entitled "Here," for instance, offers a modest prose description of a room and the furniture it holds. In prose, such descriptions serve a strictly defined purpose: they provide the backdrop against which the action will take place. At any moment the door will open, someone will enter, something will happen. In poetry, the description itself must happen. Everything is important, meaningful: the choice of images, their placement, and the shape they take in words. The description of an ordinary room becomes a discovery of that room before our eyes, the emotion accompanying that discovery becomes our own. The prose writer may slice sentences into lines with infinite care — but his prose stays prose. Worse still — nothing happens.

To Grażyna, from Starachowice

You see poetry as pure sublimity, eternity, sighs and moans — in quantities unrivaled even by fin de siècle nameday parties for young ladies. Such flourishes go nowhere with contemporary readers, nay, even your nearest and dearest will, upon hearing a single sentence, glance panic-stricken at their interlocutor and suddenly recall urgent errands in town. So, shall we take off our wings and try writing on foot?

To Zb.-P., from Lublin

Poetry always exaggerates, but we must admit that this happens less frequently now. The conceit that animates Jan Andrzej Morsztyn's sonnet "Galley Slaves" is inconceivable today: he compares love's distress to the torments of a slave chained to a galley and concludes offhandedly that the galley slaves of this earth have it easier. The sonnet is written with verve, but we doubt that anyone has ever been convinced of the author's pain. Hence the moral: we must use caution if we wish to be believed. "I weep bloody tears for you ..." Really, Mr. P.?

To P. G., from Katowice

We aren't maximalists, we don't expect great spiritual upheavals from our daily reading. Such emotions occur only rarely, and when they do, they should be viewed as gifts, not as fate's obligations. For ordinary purposes it's enough that our reading shows us the world in a light we ourselves do not generate, that it startles, unsettles, delights us for a moment. Not every poem will transport us as Mickiewicz's "Ode to Youth" once did, but each should be a surprise. Descriptors like "correct," "ordinary," "predictable" disqualify it on the spot. The attempts you've sent us show that you can write about all kinds of approved poetic topics while maintaining your emotional equilibrium. This trait is invaluable in daily life, especially while struggling to negotiate red tape. It is less useful, though, in poetry, which doesn't occur every day, just on special occasions, it is a happy accident, it sprouts under exceptional conditions. Even poets with many volumes to their credit never "get used" to writing poems.

To L. P., from Kutno

It would be pleasant and just if strength of feeling alone decided a poem's artistic worth. Petrarch would then assuredly rank far below some young fellow, let's call him Bombino, insofar as this Bombino was actually driven mad by love, while Petrarch on the other hand retained the presence of mind required to invent splendid metaphors.

To a Kaliszian, from Kalisz

To judge by our reading, you seem to reach for the pen exclusively when in an infernal mood. "Bitterness," "nothingness," "absence," "riven soul," "endless torment"—these words recur at every turn. The poems' dates reveal that they are sometimes divided by substantial intervals. We may be mistaken (in which case please forgive our indiscretion), but are these by any chance the more fortunate interludes when things go reasonably well? If so, then why don't you wish to preserve such periods in verse? And perhaps the monotony

of the efforts you've sent proceeds from the false assumption that sobbing is the only activity appropriate to true poetry? Which bard's footsteps could you possibly be following? Surely not those of the poet who described several varieties of hell and still managed to give hunter's stew its due?

To Ari, from Szczecin

"Remove reality, and you'll never do a failed painting," the famous sculptor Giacometti once said. This truly first-rate observation likewise applies to literature: Remove reality and you'll never do a failed poem ... Of course, failure can be judged only on a relative scale, which is impossible in a world of absolute freedom. If a poem lacks all contact with reality, if the author dismisses out of hand any attempt to express his relationship to the world and to himself, how do we evaluate: this is good, this is less good, this is bad? Your poems are verbal jigsaw puzzles, whose mystery and strangeness are purely accidental. We could detect no principle of association, no effort to construct consistent imagery. To say nothing of sense. "I drown in the world's sugars like a body built of starling bark" ... Mercy ...

To G. A., from Szczyrk

We're grieved that, as a longtime reader of our humble Mailbox, you understand us so little. We've never had anything against rhymed poetry and we would never ever toss poetic works into the trash simply because they rhymed "tater" with "Creator." We toss them only when that "tater," a picturesque and expressive vegetable in the proper context, is thrust into the poem with no thought for the logic of the poetic image. "Not to rhyme is woe, to rhyme is woe," as our great bard Sęp Szarzyński might have said.

To A. O. K.

Every poet understands the temptation to say it all in one poem. We caution you, though, against two paths that lead unfailingly to artistic fiasco. The first entails listing a thousand things; it packs the maximum number of elements into a single work. The second juggles several concepts ostensibly containing the greatest content within a single poem (you suggest their scope by way of capitalization), hence: Love, Life, Death, and so on. In both cases, the longed for "all" remains untamed and thrives untrammeled beyond the poem's frame.

To B. L., from Wrocław Province

The fear of straight speaking, the constant, painstaking efforts to metaphorize everything, the ceaseless need to prove you're a poet in every line: these anxieties beset every budding bard. They're curable, if caught in time. Your poems thus far resemble strained translations from direct speech into needless complication — we're tempted to ask for the originals on which this fruitless labor was based. For the moment, though, please believe us, a single metaphor organically linked to the poem's original concept is worth more than 1,500 embellishments added ex post. Please send us something new in a few months.

To Heliodor, from Przemyśl

You write, "I know my poems have many faults, but so what, I'm not going to stop and fix them now." And why is that, oh Heliodor? Perhaps because you hold poetry so sacred? Or maybe you consider it insignificant? Both ways of treating poetry are mistaken, and worse still, they free the novice poet from the necessity of working on his verses. It's pleasant and rewarding to tell our friends that the bardic spirit seized us on Friday at 2:45 p.m. and began whispering mysterious secrets in our ear with such ardor that we scarcely had time to jot them down. But at home, behind closed doors, real poets assiduously corrected, crossed out, and revised those otherworldly utterances. Spirits are fine and dandy, but even poetry has its prosaic side.

To Alcibiades, from Żywiec

The poem, prudently prefaced by three asterisks, begins as follows: "They've seized my home / refuge for fear / They've seized the air / the mold from every chamber." One thing is certain: someone is mourning, but who exactly remains unknown. "Chamber" suggests bygone times. What kind? Or maybe the action takes place today, but in an old building. It's a riddle. And who are these villains? They seized the house! They seized the air! If they seized the air, it means they subsequently died of suffocation. But seizing the air and the mold in one fell swoop: that too merits notice. Why did they take both one and the other? Four lines, and a hundred questions. A hundred? Not a one. The author himself didn't know what he meant. He's not the first, not the last. And life passes.

To R. B., from Lanckorona

The poem "Twilight" compares the heart to a baby bird. So let's say it is like a baby bird. But the next moment the heart takes a different shape, it is a float bobbing on "the surface of silence." That's not all. A sentence later it turns into an angelus bell summoning "stray thoughts." You do not pick from these proliferating similes, they are all good as long as they are "poetic." A simile serves to give a description more power and precision. If it does not perform this function, it is pointless. So what is left of a poem that compares everything to everything without a care for consistency or cohesion?

To Tad. G., from Warsaw

Working in a field quite unrelated to culture and finding yourself, as you say, "in life's second half," you occasionally seize a pen to write a poem in which various fine thoughts are aphoristically expressed.

Poetry is thus a land of inspiration after daily labors, a land where you forget your mundane troubles for a moment. The little verses that emerge possess a certain naive, childlike charm, unfettered from any specific time and the author's own personality. "Born" poets do just the opposite. For them poetry isn't recreation, a respite from life. It is life. Which is why they try to express everything you set aside: experiences, fears, complaints, questions adults ask themselves. Ready-made poetic forms don't always serve their purpose, and their aphorisms are seldom so simplehearted. They don't pretend to be younger than they are, to know less about the world than they actually do. You'd be hard put keeping up with such specialists. Just as they would be unlikely to master your complex professional tasks.

To Benigna K., from Gdańsk

A lyric poet writes chiefly about himself. Whether these poems engage others depends upon the author's personality and the scope of his experience. Your range is quite limited. Your imagination cannot make the leap into another time and space. What does Blake write? "Tyger Tyger, burning bright, / In the forests of the night; / What immortal hand or eye, / Could frame thy fearful symmetry?" What's the point in writing more if this tiger doesn't haunt our thoughts from time to time? Alongside other equally eccentric ideas apparently unrelated to our daily grind.

From Miodnica

Smooth, pleasing little poems, no complaints, but completely secondhand. They don't contain a single phrase or image whose freshness startles us. And poetry, even when it tackles well-worn themes like the glories of spring or autumn's sorrows, must make it seem like the first time, must make new lyric discoveries. Otherwise — hasn't enough been written already?

To Marek T., from Zakopane

You misunderstand poets. No poet since the dawn of time has ever counted syllables on his fingers. A poet is born with an ear. He's got to start somewhere.

To K. K., from Bytom

We take no pleasure in repeating: clichéd, immature, shapeless ... But this isn't a column for Nobel laureates, it's meant for those readying their tailcoats for Stockholm at some future date. You treat free verse as a free-for-all. This worries us. You scribble random notes which you break as the mood takes you, a few words to the left, a few to the right. But poetry (whatever we may say) is, was, and will always be a game. And as every child knows, all games have rules. So why do the grown-ups forget?

To Esko, from Sieradz

Youth is indeed a time of tribulations. And when authorial ambitions compound these troubles, an unusually sturdy constitution is required to survive. It must include persistence, industry, wide reading, powers of observation, self-irony, sensitivity, critical judgement, a sense of humor, and an abiding conviction that the world still deserves to exist, and with better luck than it has enjoyed thus far. The enclosed efforts demonstrate only the desire to write and do not as yet display the other qualities listed above. You've got your work cut out for you.

To Elżbieta G., from Warsaw

"How can I teach myself Polish literature, especially poetry?" If you don't have a high school diploma, then you should at least tackle the required curricula for literature and history. Pick up literary journals. Attend readings. Follow discussions. Seek out friends who read widely. A rather pleasant course of study, though it can't promise immediate results. Such is life. Brief, but each detail takes time.

Zdecydowany i zmysłowy

To K. K., from Katowice

A crime story no worse than those we've come across in *Reader's Weekly*. We don't sell the genre short, not least because it keeps our attention in the dentist's waiting room. But real literature begins when live characters interest us more than mysterious corpses. Best regards.

To M. G., from Wrocław

You meekly serve your apprenticeship among the poets, you mimic their tricks, you shift a few images from their poems to your own. Some poems begin by addressing a courtly "Lady" simply because this courtly "Lady" is the latest literary craze. The poems are distinguished by their careful rhymes and their author's total indifference to his chosen theme. His age explains much. At seventeen we imitate everything except ourselves. We recall those days in painful detail.

To Jawor, from Wrocław

A few pages in your story merit praise, namely, those in which the professor delivers his lecture on astrozoology. We admire the ingenuity with which you imitate the rigors of a pseudoscientific discipline. It's a shame the remaining story falls short. The literary beginner's lot is not easy. She or he is expected to provide a finished whole: a complete poem, not just a successful metaphor, a full story, not just a striking passage. Fragments, outlines, and notes are published only posthumously, after a lifetime spent struggling to achieve mastery. Please stay in touch. We sincerely hope that you'll keep writing.

To Michał, from Nowy Targ

Rilke discouraged young poets from tackling large topics: they're the hardest, and demand great artistic maturity. He recommended starting with what surrounds you, taking stock of your everyday existence, what's been lost and what's been found. He recommended writing about the things you see, images from dreams, remembered objects. "If daily life seems poor," he writes, "do not blame it; blame yourself, tell yourself that you are not poet enough to call forth its riches." Our advice may strike you as pedestrian. Hence we've called one of the world's most esoteric poets to our defense. And see how he valued so-called ordinary things.

To B. Bz., from Wrocław

We often get texts whose authors include their high school Polish grades in their letters. We then either a) respond with silence, b) give a negative assessment, or c) recommend at best that dreams of publication be deferred to a later date. So whom should the writer believe? Either the teacher or the editor must be mistaken. In fact neither is wrong. They evaluate differently because their criteria are different. The teacher praises the poem for its flawless style, fluid syntax, lucid imagery, and exemplary structure. He or she doesn't expect fresh language or original thought, since at that age personality is a work in progress and can't emerge full-blown in literary form. If we were your teacher, we too would praise your sonnets, which are perfectly constructed and show you followed the lesson. Alas, deft craftsmanship alone won't do for "mature" writing. Your topics are borrowed from romantic poetry, and the imagery is likewise secondhand. So we repeat: publication must wait. In the meantime keep minding your teacher. You'll need straight "A"s in Polish.

To Cz. B., from Łódź

Dear Czesław, we read with bated breath to see who'd done it. You kept us guessing to the end. And suddenly the deceased rises from the tomb to reveal his murderer. It came as quite a shock. We'll read whatever you send with genuine pleasure. But you'll have to wait for an honest evaluation, since all evidence suggests that your life's journey has just begun. You'll soon learn that Mme. Christie did not invent the thriller. Homer, Shakespeare, Dostoevsky, and a few others got there first. With all best wishes.

To B. K., from Radom

We guess from your penmanship that you are still fairly young and have many years ahead of you. So read good poetry and read it well, tracing the countless incarnations of every word. These are after all the same words lying dead in dictionaries or leading a gray life in daily speech. Then why do they shine like new in poems, as if the poet had just discovered them? "That's the question," as Horace used to say.

To M. M., from Wrocław

Your son, aged sixteen and a half, has taken to writing poems. He is morose, sports the beginnings of a beard, wears a large ring with a fake stone, uses rags for neckties, and carries his drafts in a violin case. You ask us specialists if this phase is unavoidable, and will it pass. Of course it will pass. The boy wants attention at any price, and at that age they think props will do the trick. We doubt, though, that the poems brought this on. Clearly it all hit at once — and will vanish with equal speed. If he really has the makings of a writer, he'll soon be struggling through another stage. He will discover that he's truly different, and this does not make life any easier. He will try desperately to change his nature, or failing that, to conceal it. Thomas Mann's *Tonio Kröger* tells this story. It's no longer just an adolescent acting out, but a question of genuine difference, the deep sensitivity that will cause so many later complications. But let's not jump the gun, let's get back to the violin case and the ring. What should the troubled parent do? The troubled parent waits patiently, recalls what he or she was like at that age, and seeks consolation in philosophy.

To Ewa, from Bytom

Who knows, perhaps poetic powers lie drowsing in your soul's depths. The fact remains that they have yet to surface. You impede them with heaps of clumsy metaphors piled so high that the world beyond them vanishes from sight. Being "poetical" is the reigning sin of novice poets. They fear simple sentences, they make things difficult for themselves and others. One in ten outgrows this phase and becomes a good poet; five quit writing completely; one switches to prose (with better results, we hope); while four keep fussing over ever more impenetrable poems. Looking back, we see our ten has suddenly become eleven. Another poet born every minute.

To Z. N-ski, from Wadowice

Once upon a time there was a nice, pretty, serious girl with an equally impressive boyfriend. They planned to marry in a couple of years and take up the same trade. Then one day the girl discovered a sensational rock band whose members performed in patterned, quilted satin dressing gowns. Happiness fled, the girl left with this group of splendidly dressed individuals to wail solos at various dance halls. Now there's a subject drawn from life. Not much authorly effort seems necessary, it should simply write itself . . . But even such stories demand careful composition and a convincing tone. You ramble, let fly with jeremiads, glare banefully when a mournful, mocking gaze would do the trick. You might even try to understand: good prose needs that too.

To Me-Lon, from Katowice

A boss turns up on the first page, so the second page must bring a secretary, which produces a wife on the third, hence a car speeds off to a nearby resort on the fourth, while on the fifth — we can't say, since all our angelic patience for "tales ripped from life" could not keep us reading. Lost in thought, we tossed a question into the interplanetary abyss: why are office romances always so flat, schematic, and lifeless? You insist that your story is "realistic." But realism doesn't consist of shopworn plots repeated endlessly in plays and movies. Just the opposite. It appears only when conventions end, and characters resembling thinking, feeling human beings enter the action. In this sense, *A Story Like Many Others* could not be further removed from realist prose. Which does not, however, bring it any closer to other types of literary fiction.

To M. O., from Trzebien

"My parting with summer springs forth like a white breast from a tunic bound with gems . . ." Many questions leap to mind: why a breast, why white, why springing, why from a tunic. The remaining poem leaves these questions unanswered. Instead Adam turns up, tempted by a snake — a bold innovation, but unlikely to catch on. Humanity has long since happily blamed it all on Eve.

To A. G. K.

A nice little story, simply told, with a single point: how pleasant it is to love and be loved at first sight, especially with no past attachments to impede you and no future obstacles in view. We'd gladly attend the wedding and raise a glass to the prospects of this well-matched pair. As readers, though, we are disappointed. The blame may lie with fairy tales read in childhood, where evil fairies work to thwart the happy ending, at least temporarily. Best wishes.

To B-dan, from Chełm, Lublin Province

You write, your letter informs us, without using a single metaphor that has previously appeared in poetry. Let's take a look. You don't use "poetic" metaphors, it's true, but the new metaphors, those you generate yourself, are likewise secondhand, taken from daily speech. You see, metaphors aren't simply a poetic affectation — they are a vital component of language as such. We are never entirely free of them. You are making unnecessary trouble for yourself in any case. The first question should always be: what do I have to say? No formal trick on earth can mask poetic vacancy. "I want to be a poet . . ."

Another false start. We favor those who simply "want to write." That's what counts.

To H. O., from Poznań

People rarely translate poetry for pleasure, especially when it comes to someone as difficult as Goethe. The translator must not only stay faithful to the text. He or she should also reveal the poem's full beauty while retaining its form and suggesting the epoch's style and spirit. In your version, Goethe becomes a writer whose odds of achieving world glory are slim. He sings his love in awkward rhymes ("to lose / in truth," "heavenly / enemy"); struggles with simple sentence structure ("when you at the market draw near"); and frequently bungles his meters. What could Mickiewicz have possibly seen in this deadbeat?

To M. Mar., from Warsaw

"Poem on My Mother" is smoothly written and polished to a high sheen. It expresses sentiments we all hold dear, for obvious reasons. Still the poem fails to move us on even the most basic level, and raises certain doubts we'll address in a moment. The template for poems about one's mother dates back at least to the nineteenth century. The young poet's parent is always a little old lady whose furrowed face is framed by a halo of gray hair. She wears a black dress and clasps her wizened, trembling hands in her lap. This model persists in poetry to this day, though the mothers of twenty-year-old upstarts are now typically in their early forties and, in cities at least, no longer view themselves as stately matrons. Indeed, they do everything possible to avoid that fate. In vain: their sons' imaginations are hopelessly clichéd. Which does not lead to the writing of good poetry.

To A. M., from Warsaw

Little children dash to school, clip clip clop, while showers patter, drip drip drop, or snowflakes pitter, plip plip plop . . . What could it be? Of course, it's poetry for children composed by awful ladies. You wish to join their ranks. We can't stop you, but we do ask you to spare our feelings, which flee such writing, hip hip hop.

To M. N., from Warsaw

"If you decide to print these poems, I've picked a pseudonym, 'Consuela Montero.' Thank you!" What lovely notions enter a thirteen-year-old head. This set us wondering: have the editors of some Spanish weekly recently received poems from the real Consuela Montero requesting the exotic pseudonym 'Marysia Nowakówna'? Now there's a true cultural exchange. It's still way too early to speak of print. We hope both young ladies will be patient and keep working.

To Janusz Brt., from Kraków

Why does Isis stride through the courtyard of Caiaphas in your poems? Why does Napoleon fall pierced by a spear? Why do columns shatter like boiling water as mortar bloodies the sands of expectation?

There's no method to your madness, Polonius might say. While chatting with Captain Cook as they gather mushrooms.

To Br. U., from Warsaw

At first glance, your poem is cutting-edge: a staggered line here; a random "and" there; no periods or commas, that's de rigueur; a few letters capitalized midphrase (that's a novelty). Once we start reading, though, the "hail of kisses," "rain of tears," and "clown's smile" stand revealed in all their antique sorrow. An Alfa Romeo won't run if its tank holds oats instead of gas.

To P-ł, from Sopot

Generations no longer talk to each other. It's a misfortune of our times. The postwar generation particularly likes to circle its wagons; its members engage only with their peers. We can't explain the causes or predict the results. One thing is certain: literature will be the poorer. Curiosity is the key to its existence. Painters can't be color blind; musicians must have an ear. Your stories are cramped, stuffy, and simplistic. There is no window on the world, hence no chance it might be opened. This is bad. A snappy style won't save you.

To L. G., from Szczecin

"Humanity's March" abounds in uplifting orders. "Forward march," "Keep watch," "Race and roar," "Strike and score," "Lay the foundations of the future." All more or less doable, if a little vague. Your acoustic effects fare worse: "So blast and blare from ear to ear." What if people took you at your word? Two billion trumpeters? We'd prefer the apocalypse, as long as it's quiet and quick.

To E. K., from Rudy Raciborskie

A science fiction story: such windfalls rarely come our way. A treat after reading forty identical poems about autumn. The story itself has a few major flaws. Still we're grateful to the author for transporting us to a time when outworn bodily organs may be replaced at will. But we foresee problems as well as possibilities. The brain exchange you describe so blithely raises certain moral questions. A dying father instructs the surgeons to transplant his own brilliant mind into his son's cranium. We worry, and not just because we don't know if the son has consented. A brain capable of hatching such plans may not—in our view—ensure the future happiness of the species. Best regards.

To Mił, from Brzesko

Authors are not required to provide nature descriptions. If you don't have anything new to add, just leave out the moonlight glistening on the water. The chapter you've sent us, moreover, deals with stealing cows. Neither the thief nor the cow he leads from the barn would be disposed to notice nature's charms.

To 3333, in Kielce

Your novella's hero is a Polish writer, masterful and adored. What popularity, prolixity and wealth! Child of fortune, fate's favorite, borne aloft by his fans from dawn to dusk, from dusk to dawn he sips mead from life's goblet. Even when his notebook goes missing (a brilliant manuscript inside), it turns up at once in some lovely maiden's hand. Dear dreamer, please write about what's happening in Kielce. Is everybody well?

To A. A., from Białystok

You draw a sharp line between ugliness and beauty. Its contours are predictable: butterflies and swallows are divine, bats and caterpillars disgusting. The reader attuned to nature will be justly aggrieved. Of course you prefer the rose's charms, but why at the nettle's expense? It too has its attractions. And monkeys? They may seem homely compared to human beings of whom we're particularly fond. But they improve next to other members of our species. Do Michèle Morgan's eyes really surpass the female baboon's in their nostalgic beauty? Poets pay attention to such things.

To L. K., outside Kraków

We've forbidden young poets to "string" anything. Once you start "stringing," what invariably follows are tears (a babe in arms sees the analogy to pearls), or days (a shopworn metaphor for monotony), or memories (typically hitched to the thread of time). We meet this phrase at every turn in your poems. This is hardly a crime against Art, which knows and tolerates epigones. It just doesn't have much use for them.

To Zb. K., from Poznań

You've managed to squeeze more lofty thoughts into three short poems than most poets manage in a lifetime. "Fatherland," "truth," "freedom," "justice": such words don't come cheap. Real blood flows in them, which ink can't counterfeit. Best let them sit until you've given them some thought.

To P. F., from Kraków

Dear Mr. P., you can't flee sentimentality by way of graphic topics. It infects all kinds of settings and plots. Sentimentality taints life, we agree. But we're not convinced that the one true act is drinking vodka, as performed in the one authentic spot, a bar. The subject and setting are increasingly popular in recent prose. We've read many chapters — some better, some worse — from this saga. Same characters, same conversations, same physiological states, same hangover. It is pure sentimentality *à rebours*. Programmatic antisentimentalism has its own conventions, which also weary us. Alas.

To Ładny, from Bydgoszcz

We're appalled by the manly brawn of your sketches and epigrams. You don't simply want the reader's laughter. He must gasp, roar, and fall to the floor clutching the tablecloth and spilling his best cherry brandy in the process. Friends unable to share his mirth would feel left out. We can't allow this.

To Kamila W.

What divides us from each other? An invisible wall. To what should modern cities be compared? Beehives or jungles. What is the void? The void is sterile. What drives editors to despair? See above.

To B. G., from Tarnów

The author's wish to leave an indelible mark on the reader is absolutely normal. The problem lies with the stylistic means chosen to achieve this end. We caution, for perhaps the seven hundred and

eighty-ninth time, that hyperbolic epithets either weaken a work or produce unintended consequences. Apocalyptic events apparently take place in your story. Your character doesn't just grasp the door-knob; he "mangles" it. The train speeds "madly"—is a disaster upon us? No indeed, we soon read that it reached the station, it is even a little late. The wind "wails wildly," a passenger feels "hell" in his soul, a girl stands on the platform like a "statue of woe," or worse, a "statue struck by lightning." After which everyone keeps on living, walking, eating, starting families, and nothing actually happens. For artistic rehab we suggest Pliny the Younger's understated portrait of a volcanic eruption.

To Kar. M., from Sędziszów

Doctors have it easy, there's always a pill to prescribe. The National Health Service has yet to suggest anything for our line of work. We recommend Polish grammar three times daily after eating.

To M. K., from Lublin

We like the literary personality these pages reveal. But they plunged us into family squabbles too petty to make for good writing. The parents insist on hanging a portrait of granny with her miniature Doberman, while the children prefer an abstract work painted by their friend: as a tragic conflict of generations it comes up short. Families always breed trouble, and we're lucky when opinions clash on art and culture alone. We're not convinced, moreover, that granny is kitsch while abstraction is great art. But we're glad to have made your acquaintance: please send us more stories.

To W. W. M., from Katowice

As a novice author, you show great strength of spirit, sending us four poems so short we read them in under a minute. But it was an interesting minute. Please send a little more next time so we may better assess your future, or your Future.

To A. K., from Zagłębie

The untitled poem is the best; it has moments of true artistic maturity. Every poem must, after all, create the impression that centuries have been waiting for just these words to meet and unite, never to be parted. Please send more, and if you're ever in Kraków, come visit our office and not just the royal tombs.

To Paw. Łuk., from Warsaw

You long to be the twentieth-century Villon. All well and good. You crave an "exciting life, full of genuine experience." "The poet," you write, "never slams on the breaks . . ." Sacred words! As long as you mean brakes. If time permits, please review a detail from Villon's life you seem to have overlooked. The great poet apparently received a bachelor's degree from the Sorbonne, from which we conclude that he was, by his age's standards, a rather well-educated young man. It must have shaped his writing. We'd bet on it.

To M. A. K., from Szczecin

You sent us the bare outline of a story. "Not so," you'll say, "I was merely discreet. A bystander can only see so much. What else do you want?" You need to be nosier. The protagonist in a psychological conflict can't be described only as "blind." "Blind" alone does not define a character. And his girlfriend? We don't know much more at the end than we did in the beginning. She fades as we turn the last page. Remember this in your next effort: the author must spy on his creations. He eavesdrops beneath the trees, peeks through curtains, opens mail, and speculates about what's left unsaid. Best regards.

To Kali, from Łódź

We hold to the old principle that the writer should know more about his characters than they do about themselves. Or at least as much. But never less. Marek quits his factory job out of nowhere: how do we explain this? No reason is given for his choice, though it marks a turning point in his life and will decide his fate. Each human act has countless causes. The author works to reveal these causes, creates a hierarchy based on their importance, and discovers new, unsuspected motivations. The most important word in our planet's lexicon is "why": we suspect this is true of other galaxies too. A writer must know and use it well. Why not start by learning something about Marek?

To Zygfryd Miel., from Gdańsk

You've got something here: a little imagination, a touch of satire, a dash of the absurd (so au courant). But you must revise your stories at least five times. Please keep in mind that Chekhov reworked each piece as many as seven times, while Thomas Mann always completed no fewer than five revisions (they'd invented the typewriter in the interim.)

To B. D. from Piastów, near Warsaw

The original sin of beginners: faith in the almighty subject. Find a subject, and the lion's share of your work is done — what remains, the actual telling, is child's play. Especially when the subject itself is so compelling: love. A young girl's love for a married man, ending in voluntary renunciation as per advice from *Women's Weekly* or *Mademoiselle*. You've got it the wrong way around. The subject is the easy part; it holds no intrinsic literary value. It must develop in a social and psychological reality based on the author's own experience and observation. Everything blurs together in your story: some town, some girl, some man. The girl's heart holds "conflicting emotions," the man "seals her lips with a kiss" ... You can go on writing this way. But you shouldn't.

To P-ł, from Lublin

Not only do we believe in love at first sight. We see it as a phenomenon of rich natural significance. You convince us that the scene you describe actually happened, not just once, and not just at that beach. The problems lie elsewhere. In the first place, the characters who interest one another so intensely do not interest us. Secondly, the author must invest the scene with a bit of his or her own wisdom, must persuade us of its importance, or failing that, its banality. That being achieved, we will skip point three.

To Belka, from Gniezno

Of course confidence is key to writing. It all depends on what kind, though, since there are two varieties. The first arises from having read too little. For lack of comparison, a first poem about spring, when even the sun shines brighter, may strike its author as a bona fide classic, soon to be followed by others. The second type can't promise sudden revelations — still it often brings better results. The would-be author acquires some familiarity with ancient and contemporary writing. Then he or she thinks: has it all been said before? In the best possible form? If not — is it my turn? This is confidence number two. Texts emerging from such assurance are worth discussing. With best wishes.

To Puszka, from Radom

Even boredom must be described with passion. This is an iron law of literature, which no -ism can supplant. You should start keeping a diary — we recommend this to all would-be writers. You'll soon see how many things happen even on days when nothing seems to be happening. If you don't find anything worth noting, no thoughts, observations, or impressions, you are left with one conclusion: you lack basic qualifications. Why not give it a try?

To Grzywa, from Zakopane

Even longhaired youths should read past poets, if only to save unnecessary labor. You might accidentally write "Prometheus Unbound," and then be crushed that someone else got there first.

To Ewus, from Chełm, Lublin Province

And so for the second time this week we are called upon to provide all necessary corrections. Literature has no use for slapdash debutants. We wonder if the Polish Olympic Committee gets similar requests: "I want to win the world championship. I hereby authorize the committee to do my training for me."

To T. W., from Kraków

Schools don't have time to teach the aesthetic analysis of literary texts. They chiefly cover a work's themes and place it in historical context. Such knowledge is vital, but won't suffice for good future readers, let alone would-be writers. Young correspondents are shocked to hear that their verses on Vietnam's horrors or rebuilding postwar Warsaw are no good. They think fine intentions preempt form. But passion for the human foot won't make a decent cobbler of you. You must also know the leather, the tools, the patterns, and so on. Artistic creation demands no less.

To Idem, from Radomsko

Talent isn't limited to "inspiration." All of us get inspired at times, but only the truly talented spend long hours over a piece of paper struggling to improve the muse's dictates. Those unwilling to take on such labors have no place in poetry. This explains a strange phenomenon: hordes of inspired versifiers and just a handful of real poets. As it was yesterday, so it is today, and will be for the foreseeable future.

To Olgierd, from Olsztyn

You may be twenty-three, but you strike us as quite adolescent. For you a poetic debut equals topping the charts with your first single. A smash hit, a frenzied public, hordes begging for autographs, interviews, your picture in the papers: poets rarely make such conquests. Their readers don't ordinarily roar like fans at rock concerts. The emotions stirred by literature these days are less violent, though

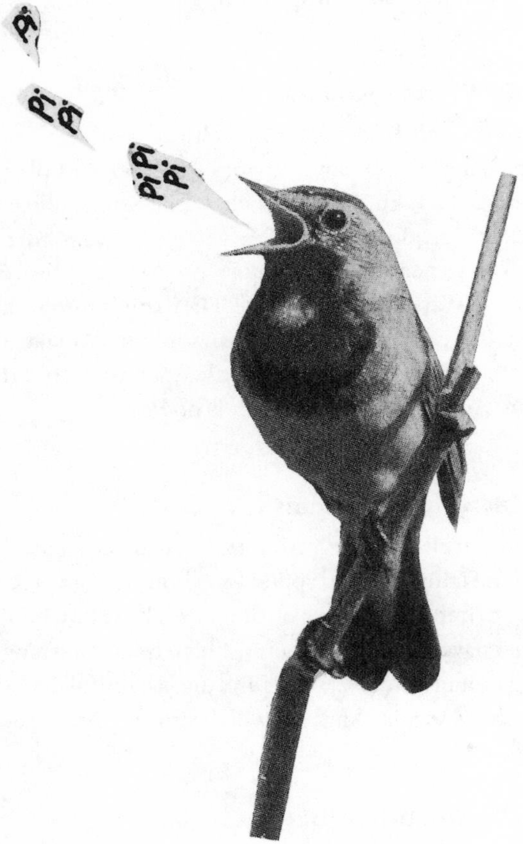
Pi
Pi Pi
Pi Pi Pi

perhaps more enduring. You see yourself surrounded by admirers, reciting poems—what poems? You have to write them first, agonizing, revising, filling wastebaskets, starting over . . . The would-be writer must see himself in humbler settings. An empty room with a piece of paper. A solitary walk. Reading someone else's book—since one's own aren't the only things worth reading. Conversations of which he is not the chief subject. Of the poems you've sent, two are more or less intelligible. The rest is monotonous chaos.

To M. J., from Warsaw

Your story is slight. You think the very phrase "great love" will do to draw the reader and win his sympathies. In fact you must demonstrate why this love was great, and why a bystander might care. Your text depicts a passion with an insufficient base and a modest superstructure. Such stories may predominate in daily life, but when literature starts taking cues from statistics, it seals its own fate.

To D. D., near Kraków

Television screenplays are written exactly like stage plays, only the scenery changes more frequently. You don't need all the technical mumbo jumbo (e.g., when the camera moves close enough to show J. Caesar's dentures, and when it pulls back so far the devil only knows which toga is which). That's the director's job, his concept, and so on. Regards.

To Pero Z., from Chełm, Lublin Province

Talking animals in literary texts face daunting expectations. They must speak sensibly, and only on important topics. The poor creatures should also be logical, astute, and witty. In short, we expect more of them—time and again—than we do of their human counterparts, who ramble and rage over pages of the typing paper currently in such short supply. We have received yet another piece in which representatives of our species exchange incoherent opinions at the Tavern Under the Bear. Please write something about teetotalers. You will find it challenging—but we promise to keep reading next time.

To Paulina, from Jelenia Góra

Fables are no longer in fashion, hence would-be fabulists require some imagination, at least in picking their animal protagonists. You feature yet another lion, another wolf, another lamb. Please include a few animals we don't find in Aesop. Perhaps bacteria?

To L. W., from Przemyśl

No, the form of your story cum moral treatise doesn't shock us. We don't aim to save the purity of past literary genres. We view each piece as a separate entity governed by its own principles and generating its own potentials. We're not grieved that your vast commentary outweighs the feeble plot. But your naivete dismays us. You praise rural life in the bosom of nature, and find the root of all evil in knowledge, curiosity, and the impulse to better our lot. We wish you greater familiarity with nature's ways and, incidentally, better handwriting.

To M. G., from Gdynia

The grotesque is a highly refined literary entertainment. As such, it demands poetry, panache, and wisdom. One more thing: it does not seek to make people queasy. All you need to achieve this effect is the sight of salesclerks cutting sausage with the same lily-white hands they use to put away the cash. Under such conditions, the written word should give comfort and consolation.

To Wojciech Z., from Kielce

With youth's carefree ease, you scribble on any subject that comes to mind. Words cascade like an avalanche in spring. Try chewing your pencil and staring out the window in despair every so often.

To Marek, from Warsaw

We automatically disqualify all poems about spring as a matter of principle. This topic no longer exists in poetry. It continues to thrive in life of course. But that is a different matter.

To B-w, from Bochnia

"In his rage he fumed like an old locomotive . . ." Not possible, since locomotives had yet to be invented. Moreoever, the sonnet you cite ostensibly dates to the seventeenth century, but its rhymes are too weak to suit that era's taste. They didn't have editors back then, but they did have standards. Please send something else down the line. For all its faults your first try has some charm.

To J. G., from the Żywiec District

As a little girl (which was not so long ago), did you like rhymes about model children who always did everything right? We did not, we scowled when forced to recite such lines. We preferred poems about less perfect children, even brats. We knew a moral would arrive in the last couplet. Who cared? The rest held fabulous adventures and forbidden joys. Do children today really have such different tastes? This would be the shock of the century.

To J. G., from Zielona Góra

The cosmic flights we will take in the year 3806 so engrossed the writer that our own planet and its daily business slipped his mind; his powers of invention were spent elsewhere. In distant times, we read with relief, we will continue to eat ice cream, listen to birds sing in the woods, and wonder why the mailman hasn't come. No pills, no automats, no robots, no screws twisted into our brains, no radar for reading people's thoughts or other atrocities that terrify older authors. Thank you, dear Jacek.

To a Thomist, from Sopot

The philosopher bore no resemblance to the feeble senior citizen you describe. He died while still in his forties, which even the Middle Ages did not consider ancient. His life, moreover, was not nearly as harmonious and sweet as your story would have it. Why did you choose a hero about whom you know so little? Prose poems are superior to such fiction if only because they can't be fact-checked. We take it on faith when apple trees bear fruit resembling the breasts of ruined maidens.

To K. W. Sz., from Bytom

Today's Mailbox brings good tidings for femmes fatales. Your novella bears the unambiguous title of *Vampiress*. This lady does indeed behave abominably. Not only does she not love her husbands. She never finishes her masterpieces or completes her discoveries. It's a shame we don't learn what these inventions and masterworks were meant to be. We'd prefer to seethe with better-motivated indignation.

To G. O.

It's true that Nero had an appalling nature, that he wallowed in debauchery and graphomania. Still he can't be accused of eating french fries. Though "the fries" and "demise" does make a lovely rhyme.

To Kali, from Katowice

So the girls in your story come straight from life, along with their author. We'll take your word for it. It's irrelevant in any case, since the quantity of girls does not always improve a work's quality. Stendhal's experience was far more limited in this regard. For all that, though, or perhaps because of it, he gave greater thought to women, distinguished one from another, and made observations on love's nature that retain their validity today. Voilà.

To Bożena W., from W.

Literature holds no love so great that it can make do without social context and other such banalities. We could complete personal data sheets for Tristan and Isolde, Karenina and Vronsky, Castorp and Mme. Chauchat, Don Quixote and Dulcinea, Romeo and Juliet. Our correspondents tend to treat love as self-sufficient. They give their couple names, provide a room and bed, and assume their readers have everything they need to comprehend this popular emotion. Such stories strain our patience.

To Hi, from Bochnia

We remained calm even when a bridge player was unmasked as the ghost of a hanged man on page seven. We've read stranger things, we've seen stranger things (to say nothing of what we've been told). We flung the story aside only upon realizing that neither the ghost nor the other three players knew the basic rules of the game. We suggest they take up dominoes.

To L. Ar., from Kraków.

Leo Tolstoy reportedly hid in a wardrobe to eavesdrop on his young relations' chatter. You could use a little of his impudence. You write about dormitory life. The narrative is well constructed, but your schoolgirls converse in the style of Madame de Lafayette's *Princesse de Clèves.* "I fear," says one young lady, "that Maciek cannot fathom my emotions." "Indeed," replies another, "he has been much distracted of late."

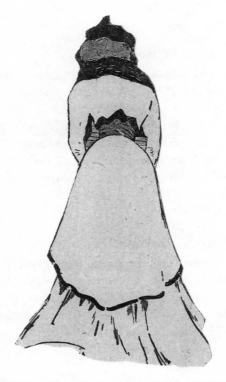

Ma, ale nie pokaże...

To W. S., from Wałbrzych

Anything goes in the world of the living: not so in the land of the dead. This region, dear Waldek, demands pedantic accuracy from the poet. You write: "Phantoms stride across black mountains, tread through fields, hurting their feet." Please! A phantom's feet cannot possibly be injured. This fact is so generally acknowledged that even encyclopedias pass over it in silence.

To Patyk, from Kielce

Margaret of Valois wore a belt with many pockets in which she kept her lovers' dried-out hearts. This did not dismay the poets of the day. They vied in writing poems woven of the subtlest compliments for this distinguished lady. Your unkind muse pales by comparison; her cruelty consists of doing the twist with other men. And what is her reward? Decidedly uncourtly poems describing the minx in language far below both social and orthographic norms. How complicated these things are.

To Leon and Timoteusz, from Łódź

The description of Grażyna and Robert in a boat meets minimal realistic expectations (however low, they never go away). We experience the hangover after mixing beer and cognac almost physiologically. Łódź's recreational resources and their topography are, moreover, impeccably rendered. For all that, though, we don't know where the heroes get their money. We don't ask because we envy their way of life; it is exceptionally dull and involves endless silly conversations, or so your story suggests. We ask because realist prose demands such information. Balzac set the standard, and it still holds today.

To Ludomir, from Olsztyn

From the verses you've sent we conclude you are in love. Someone said that every lover is a poet. This is an overstatement. We wish you success in your personal life.

To L-k B-k, from Słupsk

We require more from a self-styled Icarus than what unfolds in your protracted poem. You fail to recognize that today's Icarus rises over a very different landscape. He sees highways swarming with cars and trucks, airports with runways, large cities, extensive ports, and other such realia. Might not a jet rush past his ear at times?

To Ł. W., from Kraków

We evaluate love poems, but do not give advice in matters of the heart. Privately we'd be delighted, but this column promotes the interests of poetry, which thrives on the soil of misguided feelings and in climates fed by emotional distress. In short we wish to read good poetry, and must insist on at least one disappointment before writing. True talent will know what to do with it. With best wishes.

To M. S., from Koszalin

"I've been criticized for making my stories up and not taking them from experience. Is this correct?" No, it is not. Such doctrinaire assumptions would exclude three quarters of world literature. No writer draws on his life alone. He borrows others' experience when it suits him, and fuses it with his own — or uses his imagination. But a true artist imagines events with all the force of reality: they become personal experience. Flaubert declared he was Emma Bovary for precisely this reason. If naysayers had persuaded him that imagination was off-limits, he'd have dropped the novel in hopes that some real Madame Bovary would come along to finish it. The result would doubtless be the work of a true graphomaniac. So much for theory. When you send your stories, we will not check them against your résumé. We are literary critics, not detectives.

To Hen. Zet., from Warsaw

The women in your stories have different names, but they are otherwise identical, and identically dull. For mercy's sake, our homeland abounds in pretty women who are also courageous, intelligent, witty, and delightful conversationalists. Even as witches they far exceed the norm, and are thus highly rated on the international market. They fare worse domestically, though, and rarely feature in recent prose, which gives only sorry specimens, intellectually impoverished, emotionally stunted, and woefully low on distinguishing features. We pity the poor man who must first converse with them, then jot down these talks and send them to editors. You have talent, but no luck with women.

To El. M. T., from Poznań

The five-page poem entitled "Poet" has no literary merit. Still it shows the persistence of the legend in which the poet, beloved of the muses, strolls upon roses while enjoying all the world's abundance. Dear Ela, where did you see such a creature? Please send us the name and address of this semidivinity. We want to ask him which publisher pays solid gold for his poems, who showers him with flowers, and why he always has sweet dreams. The poets we know sleep variably, their teeth sometimes ache, their financial woes often coincide with certain unfortunate propensities. Of course some of them manage just fine, but not all the time.

To Piotr G., from Kraków

You conclude that the poet should not waste his powers wooing women. The true poet loves only his homeland. Any, shall we say, Grażyna fades by comparison with Kraków's beauty. The poet's classmates at night school fritter away their passions while the fatherland awaits, waving its fields of grain and smoking from its factory chimneys. The poet will not follow his colleagues' lead, and communicates his decision in a lengthy poem dedicated to—who else? That frivolous Grażyna. We wish you both lovely strolls through Kraków and its vicinities.

To Helena B., from Lublin

You ask which poet is considered the handsomest these days. We are pleased to inform you that Ovid still holds the crown.

To Al. M., from Poznań

"What should I say when friends tell me they can't read recent poets because they're not as good as Słowacki?" Such people probably don't like poetry anyway, which is why they see modern verse as monolithic. But we've got a scheme that should help. We start a debate at our opponents' house. When they use the bard's name to attack us, clapping our hands we exclaim: "Of course, I'd completely forgotten that poem, bring me your copy of Słowacki, and I'll check how it ends." We're used this trick three times, and three times there's not a volume of Słowacki to be found. We then smile pleasantly and bid our sheepish hosts good night.

To J. W., from Warsaw 32

Your prose is skilled, but superficial. You don't tackle the trickier issues; you don't seek to enhance the reader's psychological acuity or life experience. Hitchhiking forms your story's backdrop: let's begin there. We swear to you on our ancestors' shades that we ourselves have never hitchhiked. We were eagerly awaiting new facts or observations derived from these adventures. But you gave us nothing we couldn't have thought up ourselves. Woods like other woods, a campfire like the rest, some road, unspecified birds ... You will doubtless keep writing and some day a journal, impressed by your style, may publish your work. Time to start raising the bar.

To R. S., from Olsztyn

You attempted a rhymed history of Poland in sixteen stanzas. It is not a success. "Gauge your powers by your aims," Mickiewicz bade us. But he was a genius, and able to realize his goals. Still he failed to foresee the problems this phrase would create for Literary Mailbox.

We urge you to widen the scope of your reading. You dream of getting a typewriter; you think it would make your writing better. This is not essential. Your plan for typing out poems en masse troubles us.

To LO-FM, from Gdynia

You record the date and duration of writing, down to the half second, beneath each poem. If your data is accurate — and we have no reason to doubt it — you are surely the long-distance champion of verse. Some efforts show hints of what might have been a normal poem ("The Forest School," "Otwock," "Scherzo"). We beg you to decelerate; try spending an hour over a blank page. An extraordinary experience awaits you.

To Z. Ł., from Brzeg

Your transcription does not accurately reflect spoken French. We will provide rough guidelines. La Rouchefoucald is pronounced *Laroshfuko*, with the accent on the last syllable and a slight nod of the head. Montaigne is pronounced *Montane*, with the accent on the last syllable and genuflection on one knee. Kisses.

To Nicodemus, from Bytom

If your name is really Nicodemus, we send best wishes for your nameday, which will be next week. You may read *Bachelor's Limericks* in the company of your guests while the ladies make sandwiches in the kitchen. Call us old-fashioned, but we insist: not everything is fit for women's ears.

To Z. B., from Lubiąż

Story One: a thresher stares so intently at his lover (while mentally undressing her) that his hand catches in the machinery, which mangles it. Story Two: a madwoman drowns herself in the river because someone stole the wooden doll she loved like her own child. The

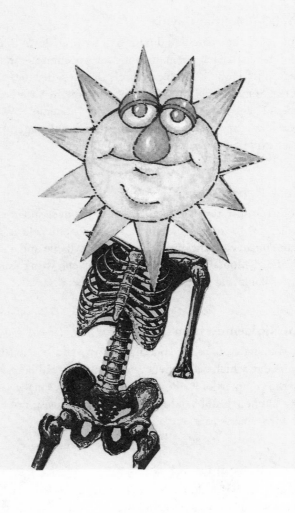

stories are brief; neither exceeds a typewritten page. We offer several other possibilities: a girl takes poison since the boy she adores shows no interest in marriage. An old lady falls under a train while handing candy to her grandson, headed for scout camp. A mailman plunges downstairs, because . . . We recognize reports of accidents in the daily paper as sources of creative inspiration: great literary works have emerged from them. Still we suggest a change of pace: try writing about yourself, your life, your own adventures.

To Merlin, from Słupsk

Poles do indeed drink foolishly and often. Does it follow, though, that the hero of every second story must be an alcoholic? You have narrative gifts. The dialogue, the situations, the appalling atmosphere — for you they come easy as pie. But we've read it all so many times, same scenery, same props, same people. You owe us a few surprises. Our humble suggestion: the hero may drink offstage, but he holds down a job in the story, and has his adventures at work. How refreshing!

To E. F., from Września

When people complain about the younger generation's lack of feeling, we smile beneath our moustaches. Professions of love engulf our office, not always skillfully expressed, but heartfelt, ardent, a matter of life and death! Who knows, when the halls are dark and empty late at night, you may catch sighs, sobs, cries of despair escaping briefly from their paper prisons. If so, your stories would shriek with the best. Death results from disappointed love in both stories. We don't dare question your choice of subject. But we offer a word of caution: the writer's psychological acuity must be equal to his heroes' tragic fate. One mystery remains: why does the unfortunate correspondent of "Lost Years" not even try to see his sweetheart? This is abnormal, and deserves further analysis. We'll pass by the second story in silence; its naivete exceeds the limits of our Mailbox.

Should you keep writing? We're sure the harshest edict could not block your flights of fancy. Carry on.

To Meri, from Kraków

Your portrait of a seance would be stronger if you showed some pity for the famous souls you summon. Socrates comes back from the afterlife to tell Zosia which number to pick in the lotto. This engages our sympathies; why bother being Socrates if the living show you no respect? We're lucky that ghosts don't exist — otherwise, posting guidelines on posthumous savoir vivre would be a matter of some urgency.

To Leo W., from Gdańsk

We like novels with digressions, especially philosophical digressions from the mind of a "devilishly gifted scientist" — as you define your hero. But the intellectual heft of these digressions is not impressive, and the scientist's mind is a sorry mess. Let's set a few simple things straight. 1) Linnaeus was Swedish, not Roman. 2) Epicurus's teachings bear no resemblance to epicureanism in its modern sense. Aspiring scholars should know this from birth, if not earlier. 3) Ptolemy was not a moron. Even wise men make mistakes. You sent only the novel's opening, and other divigations will be on their way. We thus extend a friendly word of warning: the philosophy of Descartes differs from Cartesian thought only in details. Just a precaution.

To Bożena F., from Lublin

For you Henry Wadsworth Longfellow shines bright in the poetic firmament. We do not share your view, but that's neither here nor there. We are more surprised by your own poem: delete the title, and it might describe almost any nineteenth-century poet. Take a hard look at your own work. A tribute to your favorite poet must justify your choice and stress the distinctive features that set him apart from other writers. We cherish differences, not similarities. Now for the next problem: why do writers feel compelled to mimic their hero's style? Such efforts rarely bear fruit. It's a hundred times harder to use the language of your time, to speak in your own voice without imitation. Which poet said: "Let the dead Past bury its dead?"

To Bolesław L-k, from Warsaw

Your existential woes come a little too easily. Nonstop gloom and despair quickly wear out their welcome. "Deep thought should smile," says dear Thomas (Mann, of course). We found ourselves floundering through a shallow pond while reading *Ocean*. Learn to see life as a great adventure happening to you. This is our only advice for the moment.

To the Author of *The Pianist's World*

We advise you—for a few months at least—to read only the great humorists. You won't be wasting time: such activity provides rest and recreation for a mind worn down by its own lyricism. It also demonstrates, incidentally, the folly of excessive self-importance. After this course of treatment, you will see your poems differently. The mood of *The Pianist's World* will strike you as contrived, and the metaphor "life licks us with a tongue of contrasts" will no longer fill you with writerly pride. Best regards.

To 71, from Otwock

A boy tells a girl that it's all over. "Nuclear annihilation looms," he says, "I've lost faith in everything, nothing matters, that's just how I am, goodbye." And he departs, but not for the wilderness—he's found another girl he likes better. The jilted girl begins crying. It is not self-pity. She weeps for the boy, an angst-ridden child of his times. Fine, let her cry. But you, the Author, should know better. You didn't see that Zbyszek is a rascal? The lofty rhetoric versus his real reason for leaving, the "spirit of the age" in any tricky situation: nothing here struck you as funny? The author must be wiser than his heroes, he must understand them better than they do themselves. Etch this phrase in golden letters on your soul before starting your next story. And remember: even future Nobel laureates get work rejected at first.

To P. W., from Wrocław

"I write about myself since that's all I know. I don't know anything about the guy next door who's just gone back to his darling wife and three children after a fling with the wrong girl. I'm twenty, I'm free, and I'm waiting for Mirka — she's gorgeous." You're off to a good start. For a moment we thought the narrator would keep comparing himself to his neighbor, he would view his experience from two perspectives. But no. The neighbor vanishes, and we're forced to endure more fun and games with . . . Bożena? Grażyna? Mariola? What's her name? That's it, Mirka. (We sometimes confuse gorgeous girls from the two thousand identical stories we've received.) "I write about myself since that's all I know . . ." Such knowledge is best dealt with later. Try exploring other people's lives for now. A gifted prose writer can exit his own skin at will and enter the mind of a completely different person, a co-op chairman, a circus ventriloquist, a pregnant woman, a worker honing his skills, a widower, a little girl.

To Amaba

These poems should remain in your desk drawer. The moon has bejeweled the heavens already. Madonnas have ridden carousels before. Poems have previously been woven into garlands. You've done your homework. And it shows.

To Anonymous, from Kraków

Our mundane Mailbox rarely yields such sensations. We kept turning pages; you've got a flair for narration, a transparent style, and a gift for vivid, if superficial description. We were just about to suggest your next project, an adventure tale for children, when you suddenly revealed your true ambition: a new theory of psychological prose. After many weeks of sailing, Columbus, your story's hero, doubts that he'll ever reach land. He considers abandoning his route, but a heavenly being descends to proclaim, "Sail on!" Columbus does as he is told, and eventually reaches his goal. Those poor psychologists who waste time analyzing our behavior! It's all so simple: we're moved by divine intervention. We may seem to make light of your serious effort. Dear Mr. Anonymous, please don't take it amiss. A spirit said our words might do you good.

To M. K., from Miastko

We can't assess translations without knowing the originals. Your own poems, though, don't show much promise as yet. The form may be modern, but the mood is pure fin de siècle sentimentality. "Sorrow plays / new melodies / on the keyboards of the sleeping / ego . . ." It's been ages since people wrote this way. Sensibilities change, and each new era subjects what preceded it to ruthless scrutiny, including its platitudes. Moreover, the poems you imitate were bad even then. The junkyard of literature is vast; susceptible souls may easily go astray. Many thanks for your kind letter.

To J. St., from Wrocław

The story "Caterpillar" works to create a mood of mysterious terror. We remain unmoved. You borrowed your terror from Kafka, and like so many borrowed things, it was ill-used . Thank heavens the lender does not want it back.

To Rob. W., from Białystok

No, no, no, no one writes "for himself," so why pretend? From "Joe's a dumhead" scrawled in chalk on a wall through *Joseph and His Brothers*: it all grows from the impulse to impose your ideas on others.

At most we jot down an address or two "for ourselves"; the strong-willed might also keep records of their debts.

To Z. H., from Poznań

Problems in the development of contemporary spoken Polish: this is no small matter. We were pleased to receive four hastily scrawled sheets of legal paper on the subject. The current invasion of bureaucratese troubles us too. Official terms pepper our daily speech in all the wrong ways. Such phrases are bland and impersonal by design: they aim not to sharpen our expression, but to blunt it, to maximize imprecision. We find words of foreign derivation less disturbing. Every civilized language possesses them in abundance while preserving its own distinctive properties. To take an obvious example: "After clearing it with personnel, the magazinist proceeded to eat chocolate in a kayak." The first noun is Etruscan, the second is Arabic, the third is Aztec, and the fourth is Eskimo. And yet the phrase might easily describe situations arising in Poland today.

To Dr. Ł. K.

As children we ignored poems about snowmen or scarecrows. What the lid told the pot and how the pot responded: such questions left us unmoved. We did not care who danced with the spoon and what tune the beetle played for them. Above all we despised springtime, the princess parading through the fields. We enjoyed tales of peculiar individuals, such as giants or dwarves, that truly frightened or amused us. Our tastes have remained unchanged. With apologies.

To W. H-k, from Przemyśl

We are very late responding: our Mailbox gets more letters than our column can hold. But we'll surely find a space by next year's Women's Day. You have scrupulously listed the greatest European women writers from Sappho to Hermenegilda Kociubińska. But the world doesn't end with Europe. Japan, for example, boasts legions of good women poets. Moreover, the tenth and eleventh centuries alone produced at least three brilliant women prose writers, one of whom composed the first contemporary novel, still considered a masterpiece of the Japanese tradition. This grand old crone in a kimono was known as Murasaki Shikibu; she spent time at the imperial court and kept her eyes wide open. She occupies a prime spot in the splendid anthology of Japanese literature edited by W. Kotońska. Maybe she'll get her own volume some day. With our best compliments, and then some.

To Sułtan

"The greatest poem about love / is as empty as an old tin can." Such hyperboles are currently all the rage. But we've outgrown this phase. Dozens of love lyrics spring to mind, none of which remotely resemble empty cans. "So long as men can breathe or eyes can see, / So long lives this, and this gives life to thee." Do these lines seem rusty to you?

To Maciej Jl., from Kielce

The café as the permanent address of writers "divorced from life": this topic is beloved by satirists of every stripe. It has in fact grown hackneyed and is itself "divorced from life." How strangely the world works. We know writers who have finally met their basic housing needs and now refuse to frequent cafés out of spite, lacking both time and desire. And what's so wrong with cafés for a friendly chat now and then? What would you suggest? Catching up in line while buying herring? We like myths, but only when they're Greek.

To Br. K., from Laski

Your prose poems promote the Great Poet who writes his masterworks in fits of alcoholic exaltation. We might speculate about this poet's prototype, but that's not our concern. You subscribe to the misguided notion that alcohol facilitates the act of writing, quickens the imagination, sharpens wits, and performs many other useful functions in abetting the bardic spirit. My dear Mr. K., neither your poet, nor any other personally known to us, nor indeed any poet, past or present, has ever written anything great under the immediate impact of hard liquor. All good work grows from painstaking, painful sobriety, with no pleasant buzzing in the brain. "The ideas come freely, but vodka makes my head ache," Wyspiański said. If a poet drinks, it's just between one poem and the next. This is the bitter truth. If alcohol made for great poetry, every third citizen of our nation would be at least a Horace. Thus we're called upon to demolish yet another legend. We hope you'll survive the rubble unscathed.

To W. K., from the Katowickie District

Has anyone printed a guide to public speaking that provides formulas for openings, closings, town halls, celebrations, memorials, and motions at official meetings, e.g. "May we open a window? It's getting stuffy"? We don't know. Our advice is this: Be brief. Speak only about what you know and consider important. Above all speak from your heart and head, not from notes. We've attended many funerals where simple human sentiments — "Farewell, dear friend and colleague" — came out the worse for being read. As if being dead weren't bad enough.

To W. and K., from Koszalin District

We've been called upon to resolve your literary club's dispute: should candles or light bulbs illuminate your events? We prefer the latter. We're all for atmosphere, but candles strike us as pretentious. They also suggest that going without electricity is a matter of choice and not necessity, which is not yet the case in our country. Moreover the writer will strain his eyes trying to find the next line. Finally the candlelight pointing up at his chin will instantly evoke the class enemy in virtually every Romanian motion picture. With sincere regards.

To Wald., from Warsaw

We admire your pluck, but we don't share your views. Why shouldn't women's journals give advice in matters of the heart? It's well-meant and fills a real need, to judge by the number of letters they receive. So the letters themselves don't reach the heights of *Anna Karenina*? What of it? They're Himalayas compared with what we've seen in the columns of French magazines. We once got our hands on an copy of *Elle* in which a distraught lady sought advice as follows: "I've heard that men in wartime break their vows with total strangers. With all the talk of war these days, I'm terrified my husband will betray me." Now there's a problem for you. With our compliments.

To L. O. 88, from Nowa Huta

You dismiss your current "unpoetic" occupation without even saying what you do: is it really beneath our attention? We meet with such reluctance all too frequently these days. For example, our apartment building has been a construction zone for years. Dozens of workers appear in our hallways daily. People knock, we ask "Who's there?", but no one names a profession: the plasterer, the carpenter, the locksmith, the plumber, the electrician. No, it's always "the pipes," "the wires," "the ceiling." That's a shame, since plasterers have an honorable past that "the ceiling" cannot claim. Another calling has recently fallen prey to this sense of false pride. "Mailmen" are now "postal carriers" or "correspondence distributors." Since when did "mail" become a dirty word?

To Maria Dorota

You chide us for attacking theatrical adaptations of great novels. "Shakespeare," we read, "also borrowed other people's stories." Of course. But he took worse things and made them better. Whereas our theater takes better things and makes them worse. Nowadays, as Tadeusz Różewicz remarks, even "Shakespeare gets adapted for the stage." We send regards.

To M-Ł, from Warsaw

We do not foresee a weekly column of texts composed in Esperanto: it is an artificial language without variety or dialects. No one thinks in Esperanto, no one uses it in daily life, and we doubt it will produce works of lasting value. We applaud your dream of a common human speech, but we hope it will emerge through the peaceful (God willing!) evolution of all languages. However, we do not agree that a universal language will preclude all future warfare. History and personal experience teach us otherwise. An example presents itself: Mr. A. has just punched Mr. B. outside our window, even though they both speak Polish.

To B. K. L., from Zgierz

Each time a new term becomes popular, it drives competing phrases out of business. The newcomer doesn't enhance our speech; it diminishes its flexibility and precision. Who says "numerous," "multiple" or "great" these days? No, it's just "a lot." The number of events that "occur," "ensue," or "transpire" has likewise dropped: things just "happen." To judge from your work, Polish currently employs about two hundred words. It is, in short, the most primitive language on earth. Such resources may be more than enough for some people, the composers of road signs for example. It seems to us, though, that their numbers are growing.

To Ka-ma

Betty no longer has a kitty. Now Betty possesses a cat. The career of this rather inflated "possession" grows apace. It once suggested significant, long-term ownership of some kind. Now even tram tickets are "possessed" . . . In which case, what do people simply "have" these days? We possess no clue.

To Br. Z-ki, from Gdańsk

The classic old maid was a dowryless creature doomed to wither idly at her parents' side. Paid employment was not an option, thus independence lay beyond her reach. An old maid's life was hell. Each holiday brought new humiliation, each year further eroded her hopes of marriage and motherhood. People made fun of old maids. This was laughter at another's expense, hence in very bad taste. The old maid provides comic relief in your novella *Kraków Times*. We are not amused.

To L. I. P., from Koszalin

When a famous person dies, we are swamped the next day by poems singing his / her praises. Such haste is touching and testifies to the author's sense of personal loss. Still, it raises doubts about the work's artistic value. Rush jobs make for slipshod products; exceptions are few and far between. What's the first thing to spring from your pen? Ready-made phrases, banalities, shopworn sentiments, borrowed pathos. True emotion counts for nothing when it comes wrapped in clichés. The favored cliché in such cases reads as follows: You've gone, you are no longer among us, but even so your work remains. Would-be elegists also seize the opportunity to call the departed by his / her first name, as if death conferred posthumous *Bruderschaft*. Xawery Dunikowski's recent passing inspired numerous verses in his honor. Each tribute informs him that he was or still is a great sculptor, and all of them call him Xawery. Why can't we treat poems like sculptures and take time to create a unique and lasting shape?

To Reg. L., from Kraków

The educational value of *Our Gang* is doubtful. This "gang" consists of eight friends who pester their classmate because he won't join their ranks; he prefers books and solitary walks, and routinely flees their frolics both on and off the schoolyard. The gang works to recruit him by demonstrating the many benefits of group recreation.

But the secret finally comes out: he avoids his schoolmates because he has a bad heart. You thus encourage young readers to see serious illness as the only possible reason for seeking solitude. What else could explain such behavior in a healthy boy? Your story promotes the suspect notion that introversion signals abnormality and must be stamped out at all costs. What next?

To Z. O., from Olsztyn

Free verse was around long before our journal began. As for the problem of "banality": poets have used daily speech to combat poetic clichés since time immemorial. In doing so, of course, they impose new rules and create new literary models. From which they must be subsequently freed. And so on. Finally, is assigning each work to its proper genre our highest priority? Shouldn't we occasionally read without worrying if it's true poetry or merely prose? Maybe it's just good? Maybe it's got something to say?

To Baśka

"My boyfriend says I'm too pretty to be a good poet. What do you think of the poems I sent?" We think you must be really pretty.

To Tomasz K., from Chełm, Lublin Province

"I accidentally wrote twenty poems. I'd like to see them in print . . ." Alas, the Great Pasteur was right when he said chance favors only the prepared mind. The muse seems to have caught you in a state of intellectual dishabille.

To K. T., from Łódź

"I love what is lofty and wise / I love the sky when day closes / I love your radiant eyes / Which I will turn into roses." We'd like to find out how and why you would do this.

To C. P., from Szczecin

"When it comes to the color green I'm like the lead in an erotic film. I feel a burning desire to weave the foundations of a fantastic tale dedicated to my friend, a cybernetician." These words open the chapter entitled "Black Despair." The phrase may substitute for our review.

To Roland, from the Lublin Province

The problem of life's absurdity is not addressed by rhyming "bottomless" and "sarcophagus." Sign language suits some topics best.

To T. K., from Płock

In a pinch, a story can make do with no opening or conclusion. The middle, though, is nonnegotiable.

To Elwira, from Puck

The story "Consolation" has one virtue: it wasn't written in verse. The same cannot be said of the rhymed epic entitled *The Priest and the Girl*.

To T. G., from Wrocław

"The roar of the high waterfall / enthralls me with its dark infinity / I drink at the tavern's green table / vile beer from a local brewery." True enough, Polish beer is mediocre at best.

To Honorata O.

"Oh Quixote, half-mad with solitude the executioner, even in Ophelia's arms you'll be my brother! . . ." But only if Cleopatra, whom Faust has carried off to Troy, gives her consent.

To A. K., from Słupsk

"Our island is tossed by a cyclops of passion." Unpleasant, but better than a one-eyed cyclone.

To Luda, from Wrocław

True, Éluard did not know Polish. But did you have to make it so obvious in your translations?

To Żegota, from Białystok

If we take this, please pass along Oscar Wilde's current address so we can send him the lion's share of the honorarium.

To A. S.

We learned the last lines of your poem by heart: "I love nature, it loves me / Together we will happy be." We save such phrases for a rainy day. The rest of the work was less memorable.

To A. M-K., from Wrocław.

Dear Anselm, we have read your verse,
The verdict was unanimous,
Your sentiments are virtuous,
But just a tad monotonous.

To Marcus, from Limanowa

In your poem's opening, a woman rips out the hero's bloody heart and tosses it onto a trash heap, where it is eaten by rats. In the conclusion the hero informs the woman that he'll forgive all, his heart still beats only for her. It is rare to possess a spare heart. We trust the world of science will take note.

To Pegasus, from Niepolomice

You ask in rhyme if life makes cents. Our dictionary answers in the negative.

To "Homo Sapiens," from Trzebinia

You ask our opinion of Homer. It continues to be high. Why, is there something we should know?

To Mimu, from Kraków

At first, we thought your manuscripts were in verse, but none of us could make them out. We finally took them to a pharmacist. Your prescriptions are waiting at our receptionist's desk.

To Wanda Kw., from Gdańsk

We regret to inform you that the author in question is already married. We have no idea why.

To Mr. G. Kr., from Warsaw

You need a new pen. The one you've got keeps making mistakes. It must be foreign.

To J-M. K., Myślenice

The poem you've sent is avant la lettre. "Beleive," "decieve," "adultary," "cematery": all continue to be written the old-fashioned way as far as we know. Still orthography may change and prove us wrong. We'll keep you posted.

To "Astra," from Katowice

A hundred years ago you might have received the following reply: "Boldly done, young fellow! Your verses sound a note, both plangent and new, that heralds a poetic future awash in fresh colors . . ." We no longer write this way. You've come a century too late.

To Welur, from Chełm

"Does the enclosed prose betray talent?" It does.

To Melissa V., from Kraków

In this world, everything wears out with daily use — except the rules of grammar. Feel free to use them more frequently. They'll hold up just fine.

To A. P. , from Białogard

"I sigh to be a poet." We groan to be editors at such moments.

To Karol C., from Kraków

You're right, autumn is sort of sad somehow.

To J. Grot

"Can literature help to cheer people's hearts?" Yes of course, but only when it's legibly written or typed.

To E. L., from Warsaw

Perhaps you could learn to love in prose.

To Malina Z., from Krynica

"Change as much as you want, but publish it!" We rewrote it completely and it came out "Tintern Abbey." Alas it's already been published.

To W. S., from London

It's a shame you didn't acquaint yourself with feudal Denmark's social structures before sitting down to write your tragedy. Sensation outweighs plausibility in the play. One glaring example is the Father's Ghost; without his open provocations, the whole bloody mess would have come to nothing. As materialists, we're convinced that ghosts do not tell the truth. We thus find it hard to credit any plot concocted in the afterlife; the vicissitudes that result are, to our minds, pitiful. We recommend wider reading, less writing and more local observation, and raising only questions that have answers.

Pseudo-afterword

The editor of Literary Mailbox has just left on vacation to Kashubian Switzerland and Warsaw's Italy District. Our beloved Readers have long demanded a reproduction of his likeness and some knowledge of his personal habits and traits. His brief absence at last permits us to address their heartfelt wishes.

He is tidy, pleasant, and kind. He adores animals, which alas can't be guessed from the photograph. He prizes docility in women and pluck in men. He loves history and politics, but it is not mutual. He is exceedingly sociable, which comes more easily since he never reads his colleagues' work. He is best known for a few experimental textbooks and a railroad timetable modeled on the avant-garde prose of Nathalie Sarraute. He has also published several volumes of poetry which sold out so fast that we never caught sight of the titles. Literary essays and criticism remain his strong suit. The second edition of his book on creative psychology, *How to Start and When to Stop* (State Publishing Institute, 1962) should appear shortly. He not only composed the entries on "Poetry" and "Prose" for the *Great Universal Encyclopedia*; in a fit of zeal, he penned all the entries in-between. A hefty selection of his essays, *What Every Beginning Author Ought to Know*, is now in press. He is currently working on its sequel, *What Every Beginning Authoress Ought to Know*. Illustrations will be abundant and specific.

Springtime often floods him with irrational outbursts of emotion. He then hums his favorite song, "Woman gives us fleeting pleasure, but then she bites like a grass snake . . ."

He is unmarried. Which should be obvious.

—WISŁAWA SZYMBORSKA

A conversation about the Literary Mailbox

TERESA WALAS: So who came up with the advice column at *Literary Life*?

WISŁAWA SZYMBORSKA: We didn't start from scratch. It's an old tradition in literary journals. They've always corresponded with authors, especially novices, without actually saying anything. They use shorthand: "We are unable to publish . . ." or "We recommend further revision." We decided to explain our responses now and then.

TW: We—meaning who?

WS: Włodzimierz Maciąg and I.* We took turns running the Literary Mailbox. It's easy to tell our letters apart. Maciąg used the masculine past tense, and I wrote in the first person plural. I couldn't use feminine forms since I was the only woman on the editorial board. They'd have spotted me instantly.

TW: The hangman is anonymous, he always wears a mask.

WS: Strong language. But these executions weren't fatal. The victims were free to keep writing and send their texts elsewhere. Or even to try writing a little better. Our correspondents were mainly young, when anything is possible. You might even become a real writer.

TW: You didn't feel heartless at times, crushing some timid would-be author?

WS: Heartless? My first poems and stories were bad too. I know

---

*Szymborska served on the editorial board of the Krakow-based journal *Literary Life* from 1953 to 1981. She and the novelist and critic Włodzimierz Maciąg (1925–2012) began the Literary Mailbox in 1968 and took turns answering correspondence.

firsthand the curative powers of cold water over one's head. I was brutal, though, when anyone who claimed to be a teacher used "comparisen" in a letter.

T W: Well, that's a matter of ignorance, not art.

W S: Art was rarely at stake in the Mailbox. I started with basics, I urged people to revisit their freshly written texts, to edit their own work. And I recommended regular reading. Who knows, a few may have picked up this splendid habit and continue reading books even today.

T W: Did your correspondents ever turn up at the office?

W S: No. But we didn't expect it. You outgrow your first feeble efforts, you even forget where you sent them.

T W: Were your standards carved in stone?

W S: Only in cases of acute graphomania.

T W: Graphomaniac. The word alone brands you for life. Have you noticed that other jobs badly done never meet with such contempt? To be "all thumbs" is unpleasant, but hardly devastating. An untrained plumber, a clumsy carpenter, an amateur watchmaker may live out his days without being showered by invectives. Not so the failed artist: "dabbler," "dilettante," "hack." Or the failed lover: "impotent" is as bad as "graphomaniac."

W S: Except that the "graphomaniac" can do it. He keeps on doing it. He can't stop doing it. Still I don't remember calling anyone a graphomaniac. I just tried to steer their authorial zeal in other directions. Letters, for example, or diaries, or verses composed for family and close friends.

T W: Nonprofessional writing, in other words.

W S: Exactly. It becomes a problem only when friends encourage the author of some pleasant rhyme: "Marvelous! You should publish it!" So a poem perfectly suited to its occasion—it charmed a young lady with large blue eyes—falls prey to an evil editor who does not share her admiration.

T W: It may be a sign of the times. In centuries past, reasonably educated people acquired amateur skills as a matter of course. They wrote poems, painted watercolors, played the pianoforte.

ws: But they never thought of displaying their efforts in public. Their ambitions were strictly domestic.

tw: Then writing became a profession, and romanticism raised it to new heights, with the poet holding pride of place in the artistic pantheon.

ws: Popular opinion raised the poet even higher in the unromantic era of our Mailbox. Let's not forget how bleak and dreary those days were. Each of us would attain boundless bliss by merging with the nameless masses, so we were told. Whereas in reality, we all yearn to be different, to stand out in a crowd. There weren't many choices back then. Getting your name in print was the best option.

tw: To appear on TV is the best way to "exist" these days.

ws: And answer the following question: who wrote the Sonnets? A) Mark Twain, B) Jan Kochanowski, C) William Shakespeare, D) Winnie the Pooh. Even the person who picked Twain goes home in glory. He'll get recognized on the street for a few days.

tw: Something struck me while going through the Mailbox. You're one of the few people brave enough to say that writing takes talent. Serious critics seldom use the word today. It's taboo, we pass over it in silence.

ws: And perhaps rightly so. Talent is hard to define scientifically. Which is not to say that it doesn't exist. I'm not a critic in any case, so I can take liberties. Talent . . . One person has it, another never will. But that doesn't spell defeat. You may still become a famous biochemist or discover the North Pole.

tw: The last I heard it had already been discovered.

ws: You're right, I got carried away. I just meant that literary talent is one of many gifts. You may have others.

tw: Did budding writers ever bring up unrecognized geniuses in their letters?

ws: Every now and then. But Rimbaud was our real bane. Teenagers usually knew he'd written brilliant poems by their age. So why should theirs be any worse?

tw: Did the Mailbox ever get uncensored texts, works you dismissed for political reasons?

ws: I don't remember anything like that. We got "politically incorrect" submissions from established authors, not debutants.

tw: So novice writers began by conforming, not rebelling.

ws: It's not as strange as it seems now. You just wanted to appear in print. So you studied what published authors had written, and tried to come up with something similar. Your own ideas, a personal style—these came a bit later ... And remember, this was before the underground press, which opened new doors not just for known writers, but for beginners too. Young authors could tackle topics that the censors would have blocked instantly.

tw: I'm so pleased that you're letting us publish the Mailbox. What were your thoughts on rereading it?

ws: That its didactic value is minimal, it's mainly entertainment. And I'm the chief culprit here. But you're at fault too, Teresa, since you remembered the Mailbox and hauled it up out of oblivion.

OCTOBER 2000